THE VOYEUR'S MOTEL

Also by Gay Talese

GAY TALESE

THE VOYEUR'S MOTEL

Grove Press UK

THE
VOYEUR'S
MOTEL

ONE

I KNOW a married man with two children who bought a twenty-one-room motel near Denver many years ago in order to become its resident voyeur.

With his wife nearby to assist, he cut rectangular-shaped holes in the ceilings of a dozen rooms, each hole measuring six by fourteen inches. Then he covered the openings with louvered aluminum screens that simulated ventilation grilles, but were, in fact, observation vents that allowed him, while he knelt or stood on the thickly carpeted floor of the attic, under the motel's pitched roof, to see his guests in the rooms below. He continued to watch them for decades, while keeping an almost daily written record of what he saw and heard—and never once, during all those years, was he caught.

I first became aware of this individual after receiving a hand-written, special delivery letter, without a signature, dated January 7, 1980, sent to my home in New York. It began:

Dear Mr. Talese:

Since learning of your long awaited study of coast-to-coast sex in America, which will be included in your soon to be published book, "Thy Neighbor's Wife," I feel I have important information that I could contribute to its contents or to contents of a future book.

Let me be more specific. I am the owner of a small motel, 21 units, in the Denver Metropolitan area. I have owned this motel for the past 15 years, and because of its middle-class nature, it has had the opportunity to attract people from all walks of life and obtain as its guests, a generous cross-section of the American populace. The reason for purchasing this motel, was to satisfy my voyeuristic tendencies and compelling interest in all phases of how people conduct their lives, both socially and sexually, and to answer the age old question, "of how people conduct themselves sexually in the privacy of their own bedroom."

In order to accomplish this end, I purchased this motel and managed it personally, and developed a foolproof method to be able to observe and hear the interactions of different people's lives, without their ever knowing that someone was watching. I did this purely out of my unlimited curiosity about people and not as just a deranged voyeur. This was done for the past 15 years, and I have logged an accurate record of the majority of the individuals that I watched, and compiled interesting statistics on each, i.e., what was done; what was said; their individual characteristics; age & body type; part of the country from where they came; and their sexual behavior. These individuals were from every walk of life. The businessman who takes his secretary

*to a motel during the noon hour, which is generally classified
as "hot sheet" trade in the motel business. Married couples
traveling from state to state, either on business or vacation.
Couples who aren't married, but live together. Wives who cheat
on their husbands and visa versa. Lesbianism, of which I made
a personal study because of the proximity of a U.S. Army
Hospital to the motel and the nurses & military women who
worked in the establishment. Homosexuality, of which I had little
interest, but still watched to determine motivation and procedure.
The Seventies, later part, brought another sexual deviation
forward, namely "Group Sex," which I took great interest in
watching.*

*Most people classify the foregoing as sexual deviations, but
since they are practiced so commonly by the larger proportion of
people, they should be reclassified as sexual interests. If sexual
researchers & people in general could have the ability to see into
other people's private lives and see this practiced & performed,
and to ascertain exactly how large a percentage of normal people
indulge in these so-called deviations, their minds would change
immediately.*

*I have seen most human emotions in all its humor and tragedy
carried to completion. Sexually, I have witnessed, observed and
studied the best first hand, unrehearsed, non-laboratory, sex
between couples, and most other conceivable sex deviations during
these past 15 years.*

*My main objective in wanting to provide you with this
confidential information, is the belief that it could be valuable to
people in general and sex researchers in particular.*

Additionally, I have been wanting to tell this story, but I am not talented enough and I have fears of being discovered. It is hoped that this source of information could be helpful in adding an additional perspective to your other resources in the development of your book or future books. Perhaps if you have no use for this information, you could put me in touch with someone who could use it. If you are interested in obtaining more information or would like to inspect my motel and operations, please write to my box # below, or notify me how I can contact you. Presently I cannot reveal my identity because of my business interests, but will be revealed when you can assure me that this information would be held in complete confidence.

I hope to receive a reply from you. Thank you.

> *Sincerely yours,*
> *c/o Box Holder*
> *Box 31450*
> *Aurora, Colorado*
> *80041*

After receiving this letter, I put it aside for a few days, undecided on how, or even if, I should respond. I was deeply unsettled by the way he had violated his customers' trust and invaded their privacy. And as a nonfiction writer who insists on using real names in articles and books, I knew at once that I would not accept his condition on anonymity, even though, as suggested in his letter, he had little choice. To avoid prison time, in addition to the probable lawsuits that might bankrupt him, he had to reserve for himself the privacy he denied his guests. Could such a man be a reliable source?

Still, as I reread certain of his handwritten sentences—"I did this purely out of my unlimited curiosity about people and not as just a deranged voyeur" and "I have logged an accurate record of the majority of the individuals that I watched"—I conceded that his research methods and motives were similar to my own in *Thy Neighbor's Wife*. I had, for example, privately kept notes while managing massage parlors in New York and while mingling with swingers at the nudist commune, Sandstone Retreat, in Southern California; and in my 1969 book about the *New York Times, The Kingdom and the Power*, my opening line was: "Most journalists are restless voyeurs who see the warts on the world, the imperfections in people and places." But the people I observed and reported on had given me their consent.

When I received this letter in 1980, it was six months before the publication of *Thy Neighbor's Wife*, but there had already been lots of publicity about it. The *New York Times* had a story in its edition of October 9, 1979, that the film company United Artists had just bought the film rights to the book for $2.5 million, exceeding the sum previously paid for the highest book-for-film deal: *Jaws*, which sold for $2.15 million.

Thy Neighbor's Wife had been excerpted in *Esquire* earlier in the '70s, and later written about in dozens of magazines and newspapers. It was my researching method that had attracted journalistic attention—managing massage parlors in New York, gauging the sex trade business in small and large towns throughout the Midwest, Southwest, and Deep South, and also experiencing firsthand the fact-gathering I obtained while living as a nudist for months at the Sandstone Retreat for swingers at Topanga Canyon in Los Angeles. The book, once released, shot up to the *Times* bestseller list; it remained No.1 for nine straight weeks, and sold millions of copies in the U.S. and overseas.

As to whether my correspondent in Colorado was, in his own words, "a deranged voyeur"—evocative of the Bates Motel proprietor in Alfred Hitchcock's *Psycho*; or the murderous filmmaker in Michael Powell's *Peeping Tom; or* was, instead, a harmless man of "unlimited curiosity" as represented by Jimmy Stewart's wheelchair-bound photojournalist in Hitchcock's *Rear Window* or even a simple fabulist—I could know only if I accepted the Colorado man's invitation to become personally acquainted.

Since I was planning to be in Phoenix later in the month, I decided to send him a note, with my phone number, volunteering to stop over at the Denver airport on my way back to New York, proposing that we meet at baggage claim at 4:00 p.m. on January 23. He left a message on my answering machine a few days later saying that he would be there—and he was, emerging from a crowd of waiting people and catching up with me as I approached the luggage carousel.

"Welcome to Denver," he said, smiling, while holding aloft in his left hand the note I had mailed him. "My name is Gerald Foos."

My first impression was that this amiable stranger resembled at least half of the men I had flown with in business class. Probably in his midforties, Gerald Foos was fair skinned, hazel eyed, maybe six feet tall, and slightly overweight. He wore an unbuttoned tan wool jacket and an open-collared dress shirt that seemed a size too small for his thick and heavily muscled neck. Clean-shaven, he had a full head of neatly trimmed dark hair, parted to one side; and, behind the thick frames of his horn-rimmed glasses, he projected an unvaryingly friendly expression worthy of an innkeeper.

After we had shaken hands, and had exchanged courtesies while awaiting my luggage, I accepted his invitation to be a guest at his motel for a few days.

"We'll put you in one of the rooms that doesn't provide me with viewing privileges," he said, with a lighthearted grin.

"Fine," I said, "but will I be able to join you while you watch people?"

"Yes," he said. "Maybe tonight. But only after Viola, my mother-in-law, has gone to bed. She's a widow who works with us, and she stays in one of the rooms of our apartment behind the office. My wife and I have been careful never to let her in on our secret, and the same thing goes, of course, for our children. The attic where the viewing vents are located is always locked. Only my wife and I have keys to the attic. As I mentioned in my letter, no guest has ever had a clue that they've been under observation for close to the last fifteen years."

He then removed from his breast pocket a folded piece of stationery and handed it to me. "I hope you'll not mind reading and signing this," he said. "It'll allow me to be completely frank with you, and I'll have no problem about showing you around the motel."

It was a neatly typed, one-page document stating that I would never identify him by name in my writings, nor publicly associate his motel with whatever information he shared with me, until he had granted me a waiver. It essentially repeated his concerns as expressed in his introductory letter. After reading the document, I signed it. What did it matter? I had already decided that I would not write about Gerald Foos under these restrictions. I had come to Denver merely to meet this man of "unlimited curiosity about people" and to satisfy my own unlimited curiosity about him.

When my luggage arrived he insisted on carrying it, and so I followed him through the terminal to the parking area and finally in the direction of a highly polished black Cadillac sedan. After placing my luggage in the trunk and waving me into the passenger seat, he started the engine. He responded to my favorable comment on his car by saying that he also owned a new Lincoln Continental Mark V but was mainly proud of his three aging Thunderbirds—his 1955 convertible and his '56 and '57 hardtops. He added that his wife, Donna, drove a 1957 red Mercedes-Benz 220S sedan.

"Donna and I have been married since 1960," he said, driving toward the airport's exit before entering the highway to begin our ride to the motel, located in the suburban city of Aurora. "Donna and I went to the same high school in a town called Ault, about sixty-five miles north of here. It had a population of about 1,300, mostly farmers and ranchers." His parents had a 160-acre farm and were German Americans. He described them as hardworking, trustworthy, and kindhearted people who would do anything for him—"except discuss sex." Every morning his mother dressed in the closet of his parents' bedroom, and he never witnessed either of them exhibiting an interest in sex. "And so, being very curious about sex even as an early adolescent—with all those farm animals around, how could you avoid thinking of sex?—I looked beyond my home to learn what I could about people's private lives."

He did not have far to look, he said, steering the car slowly through the commuter traffic. A farmhouse next to his parents', about seventy-five yards away, was occupied by one of his mother's younger married sisters, Katheryn. When he started watching his aunt Katheryn she was probably in her late twenties, and he described her as having "large breasts, a slim athletic body, and flaming red hair." She often walked around nude in her bedroom at night with the lights on, the shutters folded back, and he would peek in from below the windowsill—"a moth drawn to her flame"—and hide there quietly for an hour or so, watching and masturbating. "She was the reason I started masturbating."

He watched her for five or six years, and never got caught. "My mother would sometimes notice me sneaking out and she'd ask: 'Where are you going at this hour?' and I'd make some excuse like I was checking on our dogs because it sounded like coyotes were out there." Then he would sneak over to Aunt Katheryn's window, hoping she would be walking or sitting in the nude, maybe at her dressing table arranging her collection of porcelain miniature dolls from Germany, or her valuable collection of thimbles, which were kept in a wooden curio cabinet hung on the bedroom wall.

"Sometimes her husband was there, my Uncle Charlie, usually deep in sleep. He drank a lot, and I could count on him not waking up. Once, I did see them having sex, and it made me upset. I was jealous. She was *mine*, I thought. I'd seen more of her body than he had. I always thought of him as a rough character who didn't treat her right. I was in love with her."

I continued listening, without comment, although I was surprised by Gerald Foos's candor. I had known him for barely a half hour, and already he was unburdening himself to me on matters of his masturbatory fixations and origins as a voyeur. As a journalist and purveyor of my own curiosity, I do not recall meeting anyone who required less of me than he did. It had taken me years to gain the trust of mafia lieutenant Bill Bonanno, the subject of my book *Honor Thy Father*, years of writing letters, visiting his lawyer, having dinner with him "off the record." Eventually I gained his confidence, convinced him to break the mafia code of silence, and came to know his wife and children. But Gerald Foos had no such hesitation. He did all the talking while I, his safely signed confidant, sat in the car listening. The car was his confessional.

"I didn't have sex in high school," he went on, "but in those days hardly anyone did. I met my future wife there, as I said, but Donna and I didn't date. She was two years behind me. She was studious, and quiet, and pretty enough, but I was interested in one of the cheerleaders for our football team. I was a star running back. For about two years I actually went steady with this cheerleader, a beautiful girl named Barbara White. Her parents ran a diner on the main street. No sex, as I said, but we did lots of hugging and kissing after school in the front seat of my '48 Ford pickup. One night we were parked behind the pump house, on the northern end of town, and I tried pulling off her shoes. I wanted to see her feet. She had lovely hands, and a slender body—she was still wearing her cheerleader's uniform—and I just wanted to see and hold her feet. She didn't like it. When I persisted, she got real mad and jumped out of the truck. She then ripped off the chain around her neck and threw my ring at me.

"I didn't follow her home," he said. "I knew it was over. She saw me the next day in school and tried to say something, but it didn't matter. I had lost her trust. I could not win it back. Our romance was over. I was sad, confused, and a little frustrated. It was near the end of my senior year. I needed to get away. I didn't know anything about people. I decided to join the Navy."

Gerald Foos said that he spent the next four years serving in the Mediterranean and the Far East, during which time he trained as an underwater demolition specialist, and, while on shore leave, enlarged his knowledge of sex under the guidance of bar girls. "My voyeuristic attitude relaxed," Gerald later wrote. "There were a few occasions when I became a voyeur again, but usually I was participating in as many sexual adventures as possible during those years. This was a learning and experiencing time for me, and I was taking advantage of my travels with the Navy to discover as much as was possible. I was aboard ship for two years traveling from port to port and visiting every house of prostitution from the Mediterranean area to the Far East. This was excellent, but I was still searching for answers and wanted to know the complex question of what goes on in privacy. My absolute solution to happiness was to be able to invade the privacy of others without their knowing it."

But he also kept masturbating to remembrances of his aunt Katheryn, he said, adding, "There's a particular image of her, standing nude in her bedroom while fondling one of her porcelain dolls, that always remains in my head, and probably always will."

His comment reminded me of the well-known scene in the 1941 film *Citizen Kane*, in which Mr. Bernstein (played by Everett Sloane) is reminiscing to a reporter: "A fellow will remember a lot of things you wouldn't think he'd remember. You take me. One day, back in 1896, I was crossing over to Jersey on the ferry and as we pulled out, there was another ferry pulling in and on it, there was a girl waiting to get off. A white dress she had on and she was carrying a white parasol and I only saw her for one second and she didn't see me at all—but I'll bet a month hasn't gone by since that I haven't thought of that girl."

Shortly before Gerald Foos's discharge from the Navy in 1958, while he was visiting his parents in Ault, his mother said that she had recently met on Main Street one of his fellow students from high school—Donna Strong, who was now studying nursing in Denver. Gerald contacted Donna immediately (his cheerleader friend, Barbara, was already married) and soon Gerald and Donna began a relationship that led to their own marriage in 1960.

By this time Donna had a full-time nursing job at a hospital in the suburban community of Aurora, while Gerald was working as a field auditor in the Denver headquarters of Conoco. He said he was miserably employed, sitting in a cubicle each day helping to keep records of the inventory levels of oil tanks in Colorado and neighboring states. His primary escape from the tedium came during his nighttime "voyeuristic excursions" around Aurora, where he and Donna rented a third-floor apartment not far from her hospital. Often on foot, although sometimes in a car, he would cruise through neighborhoods and take advantage of certain people that he knew to be casual about lowering their window shades, or were otherwise lax about preventing intrusive views into their bedrooms. He said that he made no secret of his voyeurism to Donna.

"Even before our marriage I told her I was obsessively curious about people, and that I liked to watch them when they didn't know I was watching," he said. "I told her that I found this exciting, and it gave me a feeling of power, and I said there were lots of men like me out there." She seemed to understand this, he said, and she certainly wasn't shocked by his admissions, adding, "I think her being a nurse made it easier for me. Donna and most nurses are very open-minded people. They've seen it all—death, disease, pain, disorders of every kind, and it takes a lot to shock a nurse. At least Donna wasn't shocked." Not only that, he went on, but she even accompanied him a few times on his voyeuristic excursions, and, after an evening of sharing scenes of foreplay or lovemaking, which she found interesting if not stimulating, she asked, "Do you keep notes on what you see?" "Never thought about it," he answered. "Maybe you should," she said. "I'll think about it," he said;

and soon he started keeping a journal that, by the 1970s, would become several hundred pages in length, with nearly all of his notations centered on what he saw (and sometimes what Donna saw with him) after they had jointly purchased the Manor House Motel, on 12700 East Colfax Avenue in Aurora.

"We're now getting close to our motel," Gerald Foos said, as he continued to drive along East Colfax Avenue, passing through a white working-class neighborhood of many low-level buildings—stores, single-family residences, a trailer park, a Burger King, an auto repair shop, and an old Fox cinema house that reminded Foos of one of his favorite films, *The Last Picture Show*. Colfax was a major thoroughfare, the main east-west street in the area. Especially on its stretch in Denver, Colfax was a notorious drag, once called by *Playboy* the "longest, wickedest street in America." Gerald said that there were 250 motels along Colfax, and we also drove past the two-story Riviera Motel that Foos expressed interest in owning someday (he said he had initially visited the Riviera as a Peeping Tom, prowling along its pathways and the lighted windows of its ground-floor rooms); but instead he decided to buy the single-story Manor House because it had a pitched roof that was elevated in the center to about six feet—high enough for him to walk across the attic floor in a standing position; and, if he created inconspicuous openings in the ceilings of the guest rooms, he would be able to survey the scenes below.

And so he soon approached the Manor House's owner, an elderly man in failing health named Edward Green, and Foos rightly surmised that Mr. Green was eager to sell—and thus

Foos promptly acquired the property for $145,000. As a down payment Foos said he contributed about $25,000 that he had saved from his paternal grandfather's will and another $20,000 from the sale of a house in Aurora that Donna and he had bought during their third year of marriage.

"Donna wasn't happy-happy about giving up our house and living in the manager's quarters of the motel," he said, "but I promised her that we'd buy another house as soon as we could afford it. I also agreed that Donna wasn't going to give up her nursing career, which she loved, to work full-time behind a reception desk. So that's when I brought her mother, Viola, into the picture, to help us run the place. Donna's father had abandoned the family when Donna was a girl. He was a talented musician and also a skilled carpenter, but he drank. After we got married, he'd occasionally show up and beg her for loans that he never paid back. Once I remember him coming to our third-floor apartment, and Donna giving him every dollar in her purse, more than fifty dollars I believe. After he left, I took my binoculars and watched from the third-floor window as he crossed the street and headed into the nearest liquor store."

Foos slowed down on East Colfax Avenue, made a right turn onto Scranton Street, and then a left into the parking area of the Manor House Motel, a brick building neatly painted green that had orange doors leading into each of its twenty-one guest rooms.

"Looks like we're pretty booked up," he said, looking through the windshield and noticing that nearly all the white-lined spaces in front of the orange doors were occupied by vehicles. He then parked next to a smaller adjacent building, one consisting of a two-room office, the family quarters, and, farther back, three separate rooms with orange doors numbered "22," "23," and "24," each having a sitting area and a small kitchen.

As I followed behind Foos, who was carrying my luggage, we were greeted in the office by his wife Donna, a petite, blue-eyed blonde dressed in her nurse's uniform. After shaking hands, she explained that she was on her way to the hospital, working the night shift, but she looked forward to seeing me in the morning. Her mother, Viola, a gray-haired, bespectacled woman who was at a desk speaking on a telephone, waved and smiled in my direction, and waved again as I headed out the door with Foos, walking along a narrow stone pathway in the direction of where I would be staying, Room 24, at the far end of the smaller building.

"This place is quieter than usual," Foos said. "Neither of our children is living here now. Our son, Mark, is a freshman at the Colorado School of Mines, and Dianne, who was born with a respiratory ailment, had to drop out of high school to be treated at a clinic in the hospital. Donna visits her all the time between rounds, and I also get over there regularly, usually in the mornings."

Foos dropped my luggage in front of Room 24 and, after opening the door with the key, switched on the air conditioner and placed my luggage near the closet.

"Why don't you unpack and make yourself comfortable for a while," he said, "and in an hour I'll call and we'll go out to this great new restaurant, the Black Angus. After that, we can come back and take a little tour of the attic."

TWO

AFTER HE had handed me the room key and left, and I had finished unpacking, I began making notes of my impressions of Gerald Foos and what he had told me in the car. Even when I'm not planning to publish anything, I usually keep a written account of my daily travels and encounters with people, together with expense receipts and other documents that may be needed later for tax purposes. In what was once a wine cellar in my New York brownstone, but now serves as my workspace and storage area, there are dozens of cardboard boxes and metal cabinets filled with folders containing such material, all of it arranged in chronological order from recent days back to the mid-1950s, when I started working for the *Times*. It was the paper of record and I was a man of record. Sometimes I go back and review old records merely to refresh my memory on minor personal matters, and sometimes the material will prove to be professionally useful—as I suspected my information about Gerald Foos would be *if* he allowed me to publicly identify him.

Meanwhile, my main interest in him was not really dependent on having access to his attic. What could I see in his attic that I had not already seen as the researching writer of *Thy Neighbor's Wife* and a frequenter of Sandstone's swinging couples' ballroom? But what I hoped to gain during this visit to Colorado was his permission to read the hundreds of pages that he claimed to have written during the last fifteen years as a clandestine chronicler.

While I assumed that his account centered on what brought him sexual excitement, it was also possible that he observed and noted things that existed beyond, or in addition to, his anticipated desires. A voyeur is motivated by anticipation; he quietly invests endless hours in the hope of seeing what he hopes to see. And yet for every erotic episode he witnesses, he might be privy to multitudes of mundane and, at times, stupendously boring moments representing the daily human routine of ordinariness—of people defecating, channel surfing, snoring, primping in front of a mirror, and doing other things too tediously real for today's reality television. No one is more underpaid on an hourly basis than a voyeur.

But in addition to all this, there are times when a voyeur inadvertently serves as a social historian. This point is made in a book I had read recently called *The Other Victorians*. It was written by Steven Marcus, a biographer, essayist, and professor of literature at Columbia University. One of the main characters in Marcus's book is a nineteenth-century English gentleman who was born into an affluent upper-middle-class family and apparently overcompensated for his repressive up-bringing by having voyeuristic experiences, as well as directly intimate ones, with a vast number of women—servant girls, courtesans, other men's wives (while having a wife of his own), and at least one marchioness. Professor Marcus described this gentleman as leading a life of "stable promiscuity."

Beginning in the mid-1880s, this individual began writing a sexual memoir about his liaisons and voyeuristic recollec-tions, and a few decades later his efforts had expanded into an eleven-volume work of more than 4,000 pages. He called it *My Secret Life*.

While he concealed his identity as its author, he did arrange for it to be privately published in Amsterdam, and from there it gradually achieved notoriety as pirated editions and excerpts were circulated through the literary underground of Europe and the United States. By the mid-twentieth century, as ob-scenity laws became less oppressive, an American edition of *My Secret Life* was legally published for the first time, in 1966, by Grove Press, and it was commended by Professor Marcus as a work containing important insights and facts relevant to the social history of that period.

"In addition to presenting such facts," Marcus wrote, "*My Secret Life* shows us that amid and underneath the world of Vic-torian England as we know it—and as it tended to represent it-self to itself—a real, secret social life was being conducted, the secret life of sexuality. Every day, everywhere, people were meet-ing, encountering one another, coming together, and moving on.

And although it is true that the Victorians could not help but
know of this, almost no one was reporting on it; the social history of their own sexual experiences was not part of the Victorians' official consciousness of themselves or of their society."

Since the anonymous author of *My Secret Life* pays special attention to London's prostitutes, often presenting them
as well-rewarded pragmatists responding to the desires of
the marketplace—one prostitute had several servants and a
brougham, and earned between fifty and seventy pounds a
week—Marcus suggests that the author's sentiments and scenes
drawn from the "underbelly of the Victorian world" stood in
contrast to the more "positive values" promoted by the era's
novelists. "What Dickens does, of course, is to suppress any references to prostitutes and to censor his report on the language of
the dockside," Marcus wrote, adding, "The first thing we learn,
then, from such scenes (and there are hundreds of them in *My
Secret Life*) is what did *not* get into the Victorian novel, what was
by common consent and convention left out or suppressed."

What is also learned from the author of *My Secret Life* is
much about personal hygiene and toilet habits as practiced by
the Victorians. Before the mid-1800s, few public toilets existed
in the city, and, in such places as Hampton Court Park, men
and women would relieve their bladders in the bushes, and, in
the evenings, also in the streets.

"The police took no notice of such trifles," wrote the author, "provided it was not done in the greater thoroughfare (although I have seen at night women do it openly in the gutters
in the Strand); in the particular street I have seen them pissing

almost in rows; yet they mostly went in twos to do that job, for a woman likes a screen, one usually standing up till the other has finished, and then taking her turn."

He also reported that women did not wear undergarments, but, alas, sometime in the mid-1900s "more and more this fashion of wearing drawers seems to be spreading . . . whether lady, servant, or whore, they all wear them. I find they hinder those comfortable chance feels of bum and cunt."

The author's obsessive curiosity about women, their bodies and bodily functions, which began during his youth in the 1820s when he was surrounded by maidservants—one of whom laughingly "put her hand outside my trousers, gave my doodle a gentle pinch and kissed me"—continued throughout his lifetime and prompted him to write: "Some men—and I am one—are insatiable and could look at a cunt without taking their eyes off for a month."

Professor Marcus adds, "Another form that this impulse takes is his desire to see other people copulating; and in his later maturity he goes to great lengths and considerable expenditure to assure himself the experience of such sights. His chief visual obsession, however, is his need to see, look at, inspect, examine, and contemplate . . ." As the author himself put it: "Man cannot see too much of human nature."

While at times the author tried to restrict his attentions to a single woman—beginning with his first wife, for example, when he was twenty-six—his efforts were invariably subverted by the sight of someone new. His wife was wealthier than he was, and as he grew to become financially dependent on her she became increasingly critical of him—"She checked my smile, sneered at my past, moaned over my future . . . was loathsome to me in bed. Long I strove to do my duty, and be faithful, yet to such a pitch did my disgust at length go, that laying by her side, I had wet dreams nightly, sooner than relieve myself in her."

Five years after her death, when he was probably in his early forties, his memoir suggests that he had taken another wife and aspired to remain faithful to her. "For fifteen months, I have been contented with one woman. I love her devotedly. I would die to make her happy. . . . I have fucked at home with fury and repetition, so that no sperm should be left to rise my prick to stiffness when away from home; fucked indeed till advised by my doctor that it was as bad for her as for me." But later, with resignation, he concluded, "All is useless. The desire for change seems invincible. . . . It is constantly on me, depresses me, and I must yield."

Although his marital relationships did not produce off-spring, Professor Marcus came to believe, after reading the eleven-volume memoir, that the author "impregnated women of various kinds—servants, respectable women with whom he had affairs, courtesans whom he briefly kept. A few of these had children, the largest number procured abortion, which seems to have been fairly easy to arrange in the England of the time (he does not report on this in detail)."

Marcus also cited quotes from the author of *My Secret Life* that I thought applicable to my current subject of interest, Gerald Foos.

"Why," asked the author, "is it abominable for anyone to look at a man and woman fucking when every man, woman, and child would do so if they had the opportunity? Is copulation an improper thing to do; if not, why is it disgraceful to look at its being done?"

Since I was about to have dinner with Gerald Foos, I decided to mention Professor Marcus's book and obtain a copy for him if he had not read it. I thought it would be interesting to get Foos's twentieth-century reaction to a book that featured a nineteenth-century voyeur. I also hoped that Gerald Foos's manuscript, when and if I obtained permission to use it, would serve as a kind of sequel to *My Secret Life*.

THREE

AT THE Black Angus Steakhouse, after ordering a margarita and a sirloin, Foos promised that he would mail me a photocopy of his manuscript, although emphasizing I must be patient. For reasons of privacy, he alone would have to photocopy its hundreds of pages outside his motel, perhaps in the public library; and, since he might face limitations in time and privacy wherever he went, he preferred doing the job in small sections, each section numbering no more than fifteen or twenty pages.

"I'll try to mail you the first section in a week," he said, "but it may take six months or more before you get the entire manuscript. And again, I trust you'll keep all of this strictly private. There are hundreds of secret stories in these pages, and each lists the names and addresses of the guests, lifted from the registration forms. Donna and I got to know some of these guests personally, those who stayed with us for days at a time, and did lots of communicating with us around the front office. And sometimes we got to hear what was said about us—them talking in their bedrooms, and us listening in the attic. It wasn't all flattering."

I asked Gerald Foos if he ever felt guilty about spying on his guests. While he admitted to constant fear of being found out, he was unwilling to concede that his activities in his motel's attic brought harm to anyone. First of all, he pointed out, he was indulging his curiosity within the boundaries of his own property, and since his guests were unaware of his voyeurism, they were not affected by it. "Visit any of those old colonial mansions and you'll probably find listening places and observing holes. This is an old business, people watching, but there's no invasion of privacy if no one complains." Repeating what he had told me earlier: "I've observed hundreds of guests since owning the Manor House, and none of them knew it."

He said that it took him several months to fashion his motel's viewing vents to "foolproof perfection," using Room 6 as his laboratory, and Donna as his assistant. He initially considered having two-way mirrors in the ceilings, but dismissed the idea as too obvious and too easily detectable. "I must develop a method that will never result in a guest discovering their existence," he wrote. "A guest is entitled to his or her privacy and must never know it has been invaded." He then thought of installing faux ventilators for his viewing pleasure, but first had to hire a metalworker who would fabricate a model of what Foos had in mind—a fourteen-by-six-inch louvered screen containing a dozen slats—and then reproduce eleven more replicas of this model without the metalworker learning the true purpose of his work nor participating in its installation at the motel. Foos himself would have to provide the labor once the louvered screens were completed, although Donna volunteered to help. "I couldn't let anybody but her help me," he said, during our dinner.

One of Donna's tasks was to stand on a chair or ladder in each of the twelve designated rooms and hold overhead a louvered screen and then attempt to fit it into the fourteen-by-six-inch rectangular-shaped opening in the ceiling that Foos had created earlier using an electric-powered saw.

Meanwhile, as he lay prone on the attic floor, he extended his hands down through the opening and helped Donna hold the screen in place and then secured it with long screws that penetrated the three-quarter-inch plywood attic floor. He said that all the screws were flat-headed and were firmly secured at the pointed ends into the attic so they could not be tampered with from below by an occupant of a guest room. Three layers of shag carpeting covered the attic floor, and the nails that kept the carpeting in place were covered with rubber tips to deaden the squeaky sounds that might arise from footsteps.

The openings were placed near the foot of the bed. "The advantageous placement of the vent," he wrote, "will permit an excellent opportunity for viewing and also hearing discussions of the individual subjects. The vent will be approximately six to eight feet from the subjects."

After all of the twelve louvered screens were installed in the designated rooms, Foos asked Donna to visit each room, lie on a bed, and then glance up at the vent as he was staring down at her.

"Can you see me?" he would call down through the ventilator. If she answered, "Yes," he would come down to the room and, while standing on a ladder and using his pliers, would attempt to bend the louvered slats at such an angle that would conceal his presence in the attic while maintaining a clear view of the bedroom.

"This trial-and-error process took us weeks," Foos continued. "And it was also exhausting—with me constantly going up and down between the attic and rooms, and my hands aching from all those adjustments with my pliers, and Donna, who was helping during her free time from the hospital, was as worn out as I was. But she never complained. She showed much love for me during that time. Why would a woman help with such stuff if it wasn't for love?"

Foos said he began watching guests during the winter of 1966, and, while he was often turned-on, there were also occasions when what he saw was so uneventful that he fell asleep, slumbering for hours on the attic's thick carpeting until Donna would wake him up during one of her periodic visits, usually prior to her leaving for the evening shift at the hospital. Sometimes she came up bringing him a snack, perhaps a piece of fruit or a soda and sandwich—"I'm the only one getting room service at this motel," he told me with a smile; while at other times, though briefly and infrequently, Donna would accept his invitation to lie down next to him on the rug and watch whenever a particularly engaging erotic interlude was occurring in one of the rooms below.

"Donna was not a voyeur," he said, "but rather the devoted wife of a voyeur. And, unlike me, she grew up having a free and healthy attitude about sex, and this included having oral sex and intercourse with me in the attic sometimes during her days off from her nursing job. The attic was an extension of our bedroom," he continued. "It was a place where we could be alone when the children were around. The doors into the attic were always locked, and only we had the keys. Some couples in their homes installed mirrors on their ceilings, or watched hard-core porno while in bed, but the advantage we had while making love quietly in our attic was the possibility of peeking down on a live sex show taking place just seven or eight feet below us."

He went on to say that when Donna was not with him, if he was aroused while watching a performing couple below, he would either masturbate (he kept a hand towel nearby) or he would commit to memory what he saw and recall the stimulating imagery while making love to Donna later. "Even a sexually fulfilling marriage can use a little added spice," he said.

After we had left the Black Angus restaurant, at close to 11:00 p.m., Foos continued to talk while driving us back to the Manor House. He mentioned that a very attractive young couple had been staying at the motel for the last few days, and perhaps we would get a look at them tonight. They were from Chicago and had come to Colorado on a skiing vacation and also to visit friends in the Denver area. It was Donna who had greeted them on their arrival and registered them in Room 6. Foos said that whenever Donna was filling in for Viola at the desk, which Donna usually did in the early afternoons before going to work, she would register the more youthful and attractive guests in one of the "viewing rooms," in deference to him. Room 6 was one such room, while the nine others, lacking facilities for people watching, were saved for families or individuals or couples who were old or less physically appealing.

Foos also mentioned that he and Donna were currently building a two-story ranch house with a four-car garage within the grounds of the Aurora country club on East Cedar Avenue. He identified himself as an avid golfer regularly shooting in the low 80s, while his teenage son, Mark, was much better and potentially a top intercollegiate player.

As we approached the motel, I began to feel uneasy. I noticed that its large advertising sign near the entranceway at Colfax Avenue displayed a "No Vacancy" notice.

"That's good for us," Foos said, turning his car into the motel's driveway. "It means we can lock up for the night and not be bothered by late arrivals looking for rooms—and, for our registered guests, there's a bell and also a buzzer at the front desk that they can use if they need anything." The buzzer was also equipped to relay muted sounds into the attic, he said, and so at his own discretion he could return to the office promptly and conveniently. He could climb down from the ladder in the utility room, walk across the parking lot, and arrive at the office desk in the smaller building in less than three minutes.

After he had parked the car next to the office, we were greeted at the door by Viola, who had been on duty all evening. She handed him a pack of mail, credit card receipts, and a few phone messages, and then began briefing him on routine matters, including the maids' schedules for the rest of the week. They stood talking in front of the counter for several minutes while I sat waiting on a corner sofa. Behind me was a wall covered with framed posters of the Rocky Mountains and downtown Denver, maps of the city and state, and a couple of AAA plaques affirming the cleanliness and comfort of the Manor House Motel.

Finally, after saying goodnight to his mother-in-law, Foos turned off one of the desk lights and, after beckoning that I follow, he locked the front door. We then crossed the concrete lot, edged between some parked cars, and walked in the direction of the utility room, which was located in the center of the motel's main building.

Curtains were drawn across the large windows that fronted each of the twenty-one guest rooms at street level, and the lights glowed behind the curtains of only four or five of these rooms. I could hear the sounds of television coming from some of them, which I assumed did not bode well, knowing the preferred expectations of my host.

With the aid of his pass key, he gently nudged open the door of the utility room, which on all sides had shelves that were stacked with folded blankets, towels, and linen; while on the floor, next to a washing machine and dryer, were boxes containing bars of soap, bottles of detergent, and furniture polish. Deeper in the room, riveted into a wall, was a wooden ladder painted blue with ten parallel rounded rungs.

At his direction, after acknowledging his finger-to-lip warning that we maintain silence, I climbed the ladder behind him and paused momentarily at the landing while he went up a few feet farther to unlock the door leading into the attic. After I had followed him inside, and he had locked the door behind me, I saw in the dim light, to my left and right, sloping wooden beams that supported both sides of the motel's pitched roof; and in the middle of the attic's narrow floor, which was flanked by horizontal beams, was a carpeted catwalk about three feet wide that ran the full length of the building, extending over the ceilings of the twenty-one guest rooms.

Walking on the catwalk a few paces behind Foos, and moving in a crouched position so as to avoid hitting my head against one of the crossbeams, I then paused as Foos pointed down toward the light reflecting up from one of the viewing vents lodged within the floor a few feet ahead of us, on the right side of the catwalk. There was also light coming from a few other vents located farther away, but from these I could hear noise coming up from television sets, whereas the vent nearest us was almost soundless—except for the soft murmuring of human voices amid the vibrato of bedsprings.

I noticed what Foos was doing, and I did the same: I lowered myself to my knees and began to crawl toward the nearby lighted area, and then I stretched my neck to the maximum in order to see as much as I could while peeking down through the vent (nearly butting heads with Foos as I did so)—and finally what I saw was an attractive nude couple spread out on the bed engaged in oral sex.

I watched for several moments, and then Foos raised his head up from the vent and smiled at me while giving a thumbs-up sign. He then leaned closer to me and whispered that this was the couple from Chicago he had been talking about in the car on our way back from the restaurant.

Despite an insistent voice in my head telling me to look away, I continued to observe the slender woman performing fellatio on her partner, bending my head farther down for a closer view. As I did so, I failed to notice that my red-striped silk necktie had slipped down through the slats of the louvered screen and was now dangling into the couple's bedroom within a few yards of the young lady's head.

The only reason I became aware of my carelessness was that Gerald Foos had crawled behind me and began grabbing me up by the neck away from the vent, and then, with his free hand, pulled my tie up through the slats so swiftly and quietly that the couple below saw none of it, partly because the woman's back was to us and the man was absorbed in pleasure with his eyes closed.

The wide-eyed facial expression of Gerald Foos reflected considerable anxiety and irritation, and, though he said nothing, I felt chastened and embarrassed. If my wayward necktie had betrayed his hideaway, he could have been sued and imprisoned, and the fault would have been entirely mine. My next thought was: Why was I worried about protecting Gerald Foos? What was I doing up here, anyway? Had I become complicit in his strange and distasteful project? When he motioned that we leave the attic, I immediately obliged, following him down the ladder into the utility room, and then into the parking area.

"You must put away that tie," he said finally, escorting me toward my room. I nodded, and then wished him a good night.

FOUR

FOOS WAS up shortly after dawn on the following day, preparing to operate the morning shift in the office. He later telephoned me asking if I would like to join him for a take-out breakfast at his desk, speaking in a voice devoid of residual pique from our previous evening. When I arrived we shook hands, but he did not comment on the fact that I was not wearing a necktie. Not wearing a tie is, for me, a major concession because, as the son of a prideful tailor, I have enjoyed dressing up in suits and neckties since grade school, and being without a tie induced symptoms of being shorn of my pretense to elegance. Nevertheless, after my blunder last night, I reminded myself that I was not on home territory. I was merely a nonpaying guest in a voyeur's motel.

"Since we have some privacy here in the office," Foos said, "I'd like to give you a quick look at my manuscript." He inserted a key in the lower drawer of his desk and removed a cardboard box containing a four-inch-thick stack of handwritten pages. The yellow-lined pages had been torn out of eight-by-thirteen-inch legal pads, and, although the writing was single-spaced, it was easy to read because of Foos's excellent penmanship. I leaned across the desk to get a look at the manuscript, and saw its title on the cover page: The Voyeur's Journal.

"You probably didn't notice it last night," Foos went on, "but there's a place in the attic where I hide some small-sized pads along with pencils and two flashlights. And when I see or hear something that interests me, I'll scribble it down, and later, when I'm alone down here in the office, I'll expand on it. I usually remember things here that I'd forgotten to write when I was up there. As I said, I've been working on this journal for almost fifteen years, and as long as nobody knows that I wrote it, I'd be happy for you to read it, and I'll soon mail you the first section."

"Thank you," I said, but I wondered: Why has he put all of this in writing? Isn't it enough for a voyeur to experience pleasure and a sense of power without having to write about it? Do voyeurs sometimes need escape from prolonged solitude by exposing themselves to other people (as Foos had done first with his wife, and later me), and then seek a larger audience as an anonymous scrivener of what they've witnessed?

Professor Marcus posed similar questions in his analysis of the Victorian gentleman who wrote *My Secret Life*.

"Though the author frequently states that he is writing only for himself and expresses doubts and hesitations about showing his work to anyone . . . it is clear that none of these protestations is to be taken at face value," Marcus wrote, adding, "Had he really wanted to keep his secret life a secret he would not have put pen to paper." The author of *My Secret Life*, however, might have had other influences.

"A second reason which he occasionally brings forward is that his work is a cry in the dark," Marcus wrote, and being "aware of his isolation and of his ignorance of the sexual ideas and behavior of others, he desires to learn about them and to communicate something of himself. . . . He asks whether all men feel and behave as he does, and concludes: 'I can never know this; my experience if printed may enable others to compare as I cannot.'"

Professor Marcus went on, "We must grant a certain degree of validity to this assertion, reminding ourselves that in the nineteenth century the novel served just such a function."

During the rest of my visit to Aurora, I accompanied Foos into the attic observatory a number of additional times. As I looked through the slats, I saw mostly unhappy people watching television, complaining about minor physical ailments to one another, making unhappy references to the jobs they had, and constant complaints about money and the lack of it, the usual stuff that people say every day to one another, if they're married or otherwise in cohabitation, but is never reported upon or thought about much beyond the one-on-one relationship. To me, without the Voyeur's charged anticipation of erotic activity, it was tedium without end, the kind acted out in a motel room by normal couples every day of the year, for eternity.

When I left Denver to return home, I didn't think I'd ever see the Voyeur again, and certainly had no hope of writing about him. I knew that what he was doing was very illegal (I also wondered how legal my behavior was in doing the same thing under his roof), and I insisted I would not write about him without using his name. He knew this was impossible. We both agreed it was impossible. So I returned to New York. I had a big book to promote.

FIVE

A WEEK after I had returned home to New York, I received from Gerald Foos the opening nineteen pages of The Voyeur's Journal, which begins in 1966.

"Today was the fulfillment and realization of a dream that has constantly occupied my mind and being. Today, I purchased the Manor House Motel, and that dream has been consummated. Finally, I will be able to satisfy my constant yearning and uncontrollable desire to peer into other people's lives. My voyeuristic urges will now be placed into effect on a plane higher than anyone else has contemplated. My contemporaries would only dream of accomplishing what I am actually going to do with the facilities of the Manor House Motel."

However, it took him several months, and much frustration, before he was able to convert his attic into a viewing platform. From The Voyeur's Journal:

Nov. 18, 1966—Business has been great and I am missing observing several interesting guests, but patience has always been my watchword, and I must accomplish this task with the utmost of perfection and brilliance. The fabricating shop will have an experimental vent finished according to my specifications tomorrow. I am looking forward with great anticipation and hoping it will function properly and fit my needs.

Nov. 19, 1966—The vent doesn't work! I cut a hole in the ceiling of #6 and placed the vent in the hole and my wife, Donna, sometimes could be seen from the observation station on top. I must take the vent back and have smaller slats cut in the front and bent at a strategically engineered angle to deflect light.

Nov. 20, 1966—The sheet metal fabricating shop thinks I am building some special heat-deflecting vent. Ha!! These simple-minded 40-hour-week wonders wouldn't have the intelligence to determine what I was doing if it was revealed to them. This is costing me money rebuilding this vent, but I must have it at any cost.

Nov. 21, 1966—These idiots working for this sheet metal shop are dumb as radishes. They never think on a level higher than cigarettes or beer. "This vent will never function properly," they say. If I told them what purpose it was going to serve they probably wouldn't comprehend.

Nov. 22, 1966—I installed the vent in #6, and after several failures in fabrication, this one works perfectly and I finally have one room to be used as my personal observation laboratory. My wife, Donna, peered down the vent from the top, and I could not see her below, regardless of how close she approached the vent with her face. We checked the vent at night with the lights on and off and she could not be seen. Wonderful, I had finally developed the most appropriate method of observing guests who occupy the room without their ever being aware of the situation . . . I will have the finest laboratory in the world for observing people in their natural state, and then begin determining for myself exactly what goes on behind closed bedroom doors, both procedure and behavior.

Nov. 23, 1966—The work is exhausting! I am busy building a walkway approximately 3 feet wide down the center of the attic of The Manor House Motel . . . We will carpet the walkway to facilitate walking and crawling. Additionally, we will build the walkway wider at each vent to accommodate two persons to observe at the same time, and it will also enable exchange of quiet reserved conversation between the observers.

Nov. 24, 1966—The observation laboratory is completed and ready to be rented to a wide range of guests. My anticipation is nearing realization, and my voyeuristic tendencies and overwhelming interest in the conduct of different people's lives is about to be satisfied and materialize.

Later the same day:

Subject #1

Description: Approx. 35-year-old white male, in Denver on business. 5'10", 180 lbs, white collar, probably college educated. Wife 35 years old, 5'4", 130 lbs, pleasing plump, dark hair, Italian extraction, educated, 37-28-37.

Activity: Room #10 was rented to this couple at 7 p.m., by myself. He registered and I noticed he had class and would be a perfect subject to have the distinction of being #1. After registration, I immediately left for the observation walkway . . . It was tremendous seeing my first subjects, for the initial observation, enter the room. The subjects were represented to my vision, clearer than anticipated and it was great. I had a feeling of tremendous power and exhilaration at my accomplishment. I had accomplished what other men had only dreamed of doing and the thought of superiority and intelligence occupied my brain. A man has one life to live and with unrelenting determination and dedication, I was realizing my dream.

As I peered into the vent from my observation platform, I could see the entire motel room, and to my delight the bathroom was also viewable, together with the sink, commode, and bathtub. The view was excellent, more than I had anticipated. Viewed from the inside of the motel room, the 6"x14" vent was painted the same color as the room. Guests will probably picture it as a heat vent or foul air ejector. It appears perfectly natural in the setting that was created for it.

I could see the subjects below me, and without question they were a perfect couple to be the first to perform on the stage that was created especially for them, and many others to follow, and I would be the audience. After going to the bathroom with the door closed, she sat in front of the mirror looking at her hair and remarked she was getting grey. He was in an argumentative mood and appeared disagreeable with his assignment in Denver. The evening passed uneventful until 8:30 p.m., when she finally undressed revealing a beautiful body, slightly plump, but sexually attractive anyway. He appeared disinterested when she laid on the bed beside him, and he began smoking one cigarette after another and watching TV . . . Finally after kissing and fondling her, he quickly gained an erection and entered her in the male superior position, with little or no foreplay, and orgasmed in approximately 5 minutes. She had no orgasm and went to the bathroom to clean out the semen, immediately. They turned off the light and TV and retired for the evening without comment or conversation.

Conclusion: They are not a happy couple. He is too concerned about his position and doesn't have time for her. He is very ignorant of sexual procedure and foreplay despite his college education.

This is a very undistinguished beginning for my observation laboratory . . . I'm certain things will improve.

Things did not improve for Gerald Foos with regard to the second couple, and he did not take much space in writing about them.

Nov. 25, 1966

   Subject #2

   Description: Approx. 30-year-old black male, employment unknown, 6', 185 lbs. Female companion, 30 yrs. old, 5'5", 120 lbs, unknown employment.

   Activity: Room #4 was rented to this black male and black female companion at 1 p.m. They entered the room and were discussing his attempt to get money from his friend but so far had been unsuccessful. The entire conversation was in regard to money, either that he had coming in from sources, or obtaining from other sources . . . He brought in a pint of cheap bourbon, of which they mixed with water and drank. For the next fifteen minutes they rolled all over the bed attempting to dislodge their clothing. No conversation was present during this time. After finally getting undressed, he pulled the sheet, blanket, and bedspread over them and covered completely up to their noses. He immediately entered her and after thrusting for several minutes, the covers came down past his buttocks, but he stopped and pulled them back up over his head. He had to remain covered. After orgasm, they never cleaned up. She never went to the bathroom and he began his talk about money. They dressed and left immediately at 3 p.m.

Nov. 26, 1966

   Subject #3

   Description: Approx. 50-year-old white male, 5'6", 145 lbs, educated, well-groomed and dressed. Wife, approx. 50 years old, 5'1", 130 lbs, well-groomed and dressed, educated, graying hair black,

German extraction, visiting their son and daughter-in-law in Aurora area for Thanksgiving holidays.

Activity: Room #12 was rented to this outstanding looking older couple for a period of 3 days. I observed this couple on several different occasions, after their checking in at 4 p.m., and they were busy preparing to meet their son's wife for the first time, and from their conversation apparently didn't approve of her. They returned at midnight, and were still angry at the situation regarding their daughter-in-law and continued to discuss and ponder the idea of not telling their son how they feel. He said that their son's wife was probably "good in bed," and that is probably why he married her. [The wife] removed her clothing, unhooking her bra strap by sliding it around to the front. She removed her shoes and sprayed the interior of the shoes with some sort of deodorant. She prepared a bath, and washed her hair in the sink. After wrapping her hair in a towel she entered the bathtub and washed herself, getting up on her knees to scrub her vaginal area. After the bath, she spent 1 hour preparing her hair in rollers and primping in front of the mirror. This is a 50-year-old woman! Imagine the hours she has wasted in her lifetime. By this time her husband is asleep and no sex transpired tonight. . . .

The next morning at 9 a.m., I observed her giving him oral sex to completion, with the sperm running down her cheek. She went through complete orgasm without any assistance from him.

Observed them the following 2 days, and they enjoyed a combination of intercourse and oral sex on another occasion.

Conclusion: Educated, upper-middle-class older couple who enjoy a tremendous sex life.

SIX

BETWEEN THE Thanksgiving and Christmas holidays of 1966, Gerald Foos spent enough time in his attic to observe forty-six of his guests participating in some form of sexual activity, at times singularly, at times with a partner, and, on one occasion, with two partners.

Despite his many years as a freelance voyeur prior to buying the motel, Foos had no previous experience watching a threesome in action, and so during the late afternoon of December 15, he did not anticipate anything uncommon when two neatly attired men and a woman approached him at the registration desk and requested a single room for the evening.

"The furnace in our home just stopped working, and my wife here is freezing," volunteered the larger man, a broad-shouldered, red-haired individual in his early thirties who wore a tan suede sports jacket over a maroon turtlenecked sweater. The woman smiled, while the younger man stood behind the couple saying nothing.

After the red-haired man had signed the register, listing his name and that of his wife's while ignoring their companion's, Foos's instinct was to say something, but resisted when the woman requested that he recommend the name of a nearby restaurant. Foos assumed that the three of them would soon be going out to dinner but only the couple would be returning later to spend the night. After handing them the key to Room 9, Foos watched as they turned and walked toward the main building, each carrying an overnight bag. Checking the registration form, he noticed that the red-haired man had listed as his home address the name and location of a vacuum cleaner retail store located in downtown Denver.

Since Viola was still on duty, Foos quickly excused himself and went to the attic, positioning himself above Room 9 and writing on a notepad what he saw.

They were a very polite, very organized couple with male companion. The husband immediately took off all his clothes, except his shorts. His wife disrobed and so did the male companion, who revealed a large penis of at least 8" to 10". The husband was interested in taking pictures of his wife sucking the large penis and holding it in her hand.

They then proceeded to have intercourse in several different positions while the husband continued to take pictures and also was beginning to masturbate during the progress of the act. They assumed the female-superior position and the husband got real close to the plunging penis and exclaimed, "You have such a nice big cock and I love to see it go in and out." The husband was now more actively engaged in masturbation and reached orgasm at the same time as his wife and their companion. Then the husband said: "Hold it right there, and don't withdraw your cock until I get my camera ready." He took several pictures of the companion's penis still embedded in his wife's vagina, with the semen running down. For a while they all three laid quiet on the bed and relaxed, discussing vacuum cleaner sales. The companion apparently works as a sales rep for the vacuum cleaner firm that the husband and wife operate. Later, the three of them got dressed and left.

And so I have seen my first episode of "threesome sex," which enables this husband to fulfill his voyeur's drive. I could completely envision myself playing the husband's role, and I would definitely like to explore the possibilities of seeing this transpire in my life. I would really like to participate, and it displeases me that, at present, I must remain an observer. Incidentally, this was the largest penis that I have seen so far.

On the following evening, two young women from Vallejo, California, both of them schoolteachers attending a seminar in Denver, arrived at the Manor House Motel and were welcomed by Gerald Foos. After assigning them to Room 5, which had two double beds, he provided them with local maps and sightseeing brochures, and then escorted them to their room in the main building while carrying their luggage. Before closing their door and issuing them two keys, he assured them that he was always available for further assistance, and then after saying goodnight, he headed over to the utility room and the ladder leading up to his viewing platform and writing pad.

They are very appealing young women, one a buxom blonde standing about 5'8" and 120 lbs, and the other a brunette at 5'3" and 110 lbs. After a while they had removed their clothes and the blonde was giving the other a massage, and this slowly led to lovemaking that is so different from what I see when women are with men. With women the physical actions are more mutual. Technically, women do together what male and females do—touch and kiss and caress one another, except there is no penis. I've yet to observe lesbians who use a dildo. I think a dildo is a big male porno trip.

The blonde is now deep mouth kissing the other, and she is also touching her very lightly with her tongue and hands all over her body, especially her buttocks and lower abdomen. The blonde is giving her clitoral stimulation with her fingers and is now using her mouth and tongue. This continued for some time with a gentleness of unhurried emotion and either her tongue was gently flicking her clitoris, or her mouth was sucking hard, and then finally her right index fingers moving right above her clitoris in an increasingly rapid up and down movement, made her orgasm. And immediately upon orgasm, the blonde lowered her mouth and lips to the brunette's vagina and shook her head rapidly from side to side which produced an even greater orgasm for the brunette woman.

After a period of quiet conversation, the smaller woman, the brunette, began caressing the blonde woman's breasts and exploring the nipple area and said, "I love to suck your breasts, and I love the salty taste of perspiration on them."

"Do they taste salty?" the other asked. "Yes," said the brunette. "Yours don't," said the blonde, "but I guess I get more excited than you do."

They spent anywhere from three to five hours caressing, touching, cuddling, hugging, lip kissing, deep kissing, clitoral stimulation, both manual and oral and intimate conversation before, in between and after sex.

Conclusion: I am continually impressed with the warm, loving relationships that I have regularly seen between lesbian women. Their feeling of sympathy, compassion, and understanding far exceeds the relationship of men and women. Sex is not just sex, no matter whether hetero or homo. It has to do more with the way men are brought up to regard their bodies, touching and sensuality, versus the way women learn to do this. These women could sum it up with a phrase "make love with" instead of "make love to." Unfortunately, the majority of men I've observed are concerned with their own pleasure rather than the women's. There is far less emotional love than just physical love. Lesbians, on the other hand, are better lovers to each other; they know what their partner wants and most of all there is an emotional closeness that can never be matched by a man. More tenderness, more consideration and understanding of feelings, etc.

There is not any particular procedure only, and most important of all, usually either finger-clitoral stimulation or cunnilingus to produce guaranteed orgasm at some point. Women seem to

*have a more sustained energy level after orgasm. And it isn't nec-
essarily over automatically because somebody orgasms. These two
subjects appear to live a happy fulfilled life; however, some of their
conversation that I've overheard indicates that they feel somewhat
uncomfortable with their peers back home, and are feeling a little
pressure or fear as a result of their interactions as schoolteachers.*

The two schoolteachers were the only lesbian lovers who
stayed at the Manor House during the final weeks of 1966, and
the trio from the vacuum cleaner company represented the motel's first example of group sex Foos recorded, which he described
in his report as "kinky." Within a few years, however, as group
sex became more popular and the Sexual Revolution received
wide coverage in the media, additional bed partners would no
longer be regarded as abnormal or "kinky." This raised a finan-
cial question at Foos's motel: Should he charge higher room rates
for threesomes or foursomes than he did for couples?

As it was, extra charges were only levied on guests who
checked in with pets, but such increases—a fifteen-dollar-a-day
pet fee—were reimbursed when the guests checked out *if* the
pets had caused no damage to the room's interior or added to the
burdens of the chambermaid. Still, it was with limited enthusi-
asm that Gerald Foos greeted arriving guests accompanied by
dogs, and this was certainly true when a middle-aged vacationing couple from Atlanta arrived holding on to the leash of a large
and lively hound.

Under normal circumstances, Foos would have assigned
this presentable but unexceptional-looking couple to a room

without viewing vents, for nothing about either individual engaged his sexual curiosity; but Foos's prudent nature inclined him to regard their dog differently. He should be watched, Foos decided, and so after the couple had agreed to the payment policy on pets, they received a key to Room 4.

Later, in the attic, after Foos had spent an hour watching as the dog tried to sleep amid the argumentative voices of his masters, Foos wrote in The Voyeur's Journal:

> *During observation this evening, I see the same disgusting pattern repeating itself with these people.*
>
> *First, there is the disagreement over how much money they have spent on vacation; and how much is left!*
>
> *Then there is the wife bickering over how they are wasting time, not seeing the proper attractions, and all they do when they go on vacation is watch TV! Then, the wife complains about the room and why they have to stay in this dump, instead of some large tourist hotel. This infuriates me to a degree when someone refers to my motel as a dump! It is not first-class, but it is clean, and has had guests from all walks of life. She is just trying to pick a fight with her husband, but he is a passive individual and shows little or no emotion regarding her insults. She accuses him of not accomplishing anything as a social worker, and says he will never make enough money to please her doing "this stupid work."*
>
> *Shortly thereafter, I notice the hound smelling around behind the large chair in the room and he proceeds to do his duty in a large pile behind the chair.*

The subjects notice the hound's achievement, and make an effort to remove the excrement from the carpet. She says, "The manager will never know the dog went behind the chair, because the chair covers it, and besides, we've cleaned it so good he will never see it." She goes on to say: "The last motel we stayed in never found out that he went on the carpet."

After this episode they retired to the bed, and were able to accomplish nothing except endless arguments between TV commercials. The next morning at 10 a.m. they came down to the office for their pet deposit. At this time, I asked them to accompany me to the room and proceeded with my inspection. I removed the large chair from the corner of the room, and pointed to an area of the carpet where I had seen their hound relieve himself last evening.

I said, "See that spot?" They said, "No!" I said, "Your dog soiled the rug here, and I will have to shampoo the entire carpet because you allowed your dog to dirty the room." They appeared stunned, but didn't resist at the idea of the motel keeping the deposit. Before they checked out, I was up in the observation platform to listen to their critique. They were immersed in a discussion of how I knew the exact position their hound had relieved himself.

They couldn't believe it—maybe I had an extraordinary sense of smell, they pondered. Or perhaps I was gifted with extrasensory perception. "His eyes must be able to see spots that we can't see," they assumed. "Maybe," he said, "he is able to look in that window somehow, and was able to see the dog dirty the carpet." She said, "He's just a dumb-idiot manager who probably keeps all deposits for himself anyway, and was just lucky in

pointing out a particular spot on the carpet." With that state-
ment, they departed the motel, with only the Voyeur knowing the
correct presentation of facts and with a gentle chuckle emerging
from within.

Conclusion: My observations indicate that the majority of
vacationers spend their time in misery. They fight about money;
where to visit; where to eat; where to stay; all their aggressions
somehow are immeasurably increased, and this is the time they
discover they are not properly matched. Women especially have a
difficult time adjusting to both the new surroundings and their
husbands. Vacations produce all the anxieties within mankind to
come forward during this time, and to perpetuate the worst of
emotions. Most of these people seem to be very content when they
are together in the motel's office, paying for another day at the
motel or while picking up literature and brochures.

You can never really determine during their appearances in
public that their private life is full of hell and unhappiness. I have
pondered why it is absolutely mandatory for people to guard with
all secrecy and never let it be known that their personal lives are
unhappy and deplorable. This is the "plight of the human corpus,"
and I'm sure provides the answer that if the misery of mankind
were revealed all together spontaneously, mass genocide might cor-
respondently follow.

SEVEN

A LARGE building complex within walking distance of the Manor House Motel was the Fitzsimons Army Medical Center, where President Dwight D. Eisenhower spent seven weeks recovering from his heart attack in 1955. During the 1960s and '70s it served as a temporary home for hundreds of injured Vietnam War veterans. Gerald Foos was only moderately against the war when he first built his observation platform in 1966, but as the war continued, he became deeply disturbed because he frequently saw for himself how painful and humiliating it was for crippled soldiers to have sex, or attempt to have sex, with their wives or girlfriends whenever they rented space for a day or more at his motel. In The Voyeur's Journal, on June 15, 1970, he wrote:

> *Checked into Room 4 this white male serviceman, who is in his early twenties and confined to a wheelchair, having lost his right*

leg in Vietnam. He was accompanied by his wife, also in her early twenties, about 5'3", slim, and very pretty. She had come from their home in Michigan to visit him, after he had received a brief release from Fitzsimons. They rented the room for five days.

Upon the initial observation, the male subject was still very upset and stressed regarding the loss of his right leg, below the knee, and is experiencing great difficulty in adjusting to his artificial leg. When the subject removed the artificial leg, the stub was completely raw, sore and open, and was causing him great pain and discomfort. . . .

The subject went into great detail expressing how the service and society had forgotten men like him, and that the war in Vietnam was a terrible waste of men and materials. His wife agreed with him, and said, "Why didn't you go to Canada like Mike did?"

He said, "I definitely would have gone to Canada if I knew beforehand that the service was going to lie and misrepresent the facts, but I was too hung up on home, family, and country and lost perspective of the real issues."

Later that evening the voyeur from the observation vent observed them in the process of love-making. She opened two bottles of coke and handed him his drink and then she sat on the chair facing him, tucking up her legs, her mini-shift riding up and giving him and the Voyeur a clear view of her curvaceously tapered thighs. She was not wearing any underpants. . . .

The male subject smiled in lewd appreciation, and hoisting his glass in toast, said, "Here's to what makes the world go round!"

"Sex . . . ?" She smiled.

"No! Money! It's the one thing people will do almost anything for. What do you think we are at war in Vietnam for? It is for the god-damned money."

He took her, solidly, into his arms, and his lips sought for and found hers, and it was her moist, pink lips that came surging onto his mouth, searchingly, as his hands began to explore the soft contours of her body. Cupping the resilient mount of a small sculptured breast through the soft material of her dress, he kneaded it softly, and the natural and normal reactions began to materialize.

The male subject slid his hand down across her flat stomach, then out along the smooth, whiteness of a finely tapered thigh, then he went under the short length of her dress, allowing his hand to massage and caress the curling fleeciness of her pubic hair. . . . The voyeur could see the erotic spasms of her body, and the tiny undulations of her loins up against his taunting fingers. He removed her mini-sheath to reveal the curves of her soft, small, womanly body. Her legs were splayed, obscenely, to the delight of the observing Voyeur. . . . Quickly, the male subject shed his clothing, leaving only his shorts to cover him, partially. Inside his shorts, his massive erection was stirring. . . . Frantically, the male subject flexed his pelvis in between her thighs, and he removed his penis from the leg of his shorts, and in one powerful smooth thrust, he rammed his penis deep into her clasping vagina. . . .

Several strokes later, the male subject's orgasm came to him. With a groan, he slumped on top of her . . . She did not reach orgasm and was definitely unhappy about the disturbing situation. He rolled away from her to his side, and quickly scrambled off *the bed on one leg. He said, "I hope you remember when I had two good legs." . . .*

The Voyeur observed this couple periodically from time to time during the next five days, and they did not reconcile or adapt to the male subject's losing his leg. It was hampering their relationship, and I believe his wife will never accept his disability, and this would eventually lead to divorce.

A few years later, another wounded veteran—this one a paraplegic—checked in to the Manor House with his wife. Foos watched as the wife tried to help her husband out of his wheelchair and onto the bed.

But he said sharply, "I can handle it. I don't want any help or assistance." He took off his shoes and trousers and said, "here you can empty my bag." He apparently had no bladder control and had to be catheterized. She unhooked the tube connected to his penis and emptied the bag in the toilet. She then reattached the bag.

She undressed and . . . held her breasts up in front of his face for observation, and he responded by gently kissing and sucking them. She said, "I have to take a shower." During her shower, he remained motionless and watched TV. When she finished with her shower, she reclined on the bed beside him and laid real close, hugging and kissing him.

He said, "Why do you continue to love me when I'm in this condition?" She said, "because you are still the person I married, and I remember our vows, in sickness and health."

He kissed her deeply, saying, "if it wasn't for you, I don't think I could survive."

The wife proceeded to unhook his catheter and masturbate him to erection.

She rested her head on his abdomen, and began to carefully lick and suck his penis taking the entire shaft into her mouth. She did this for the better part of an hour and he definitely seemed to be able to have some perception of feeling, because he was getting the sexual pleasure facial expression and sticking his tongue out and licking his lips. She mounted him in the female superior position, and reached her own orgasm simultaneous with his. . . .

Conclusion: Because of the close proximity of Fitzsimons Army Hospital to the motel, I have had the opportunity to observe many of the deplorable and regrettable tragedies of the Vietnam War. This subject is lucky. He has a loving and understanding wife.

He will probably survive, but what becomes of the other hundreds of individuals who have no one? Observation of these sorrowful and disastrous subjects is a very difficult and unpleasant task, and consequently, all that remains is regret and pity. There is nothing more disturbing than hearing a subject disclose that he has been betrayed by his country.

EIGHT

THE VICTORIAN gentleman's intent in *My Secret Life* was to write, as he himself explained, "without any regard for what the world calls decency," and, while researching his memoir, he had what Professor Marcus called "a Leopold Bloomish experience—he spends some time spying on women defecating and urinating."

After I had read the first three or four sections of Foos's *The Voyeur's Journal*—he continued to send installments of the journal through the winter and spring of 1980—it seemed that, like the Victorian gentleman, Foos had great interest in trespassing and reporting on what occurs within the most private domain of daily activity: the bathroom.

Donna checked in this attractive young lady from Lemon, Colorado, who said her husband was attending an Army Reserve gathering in town and they would be needing accommodations for the evening. She was assigned to Room 6.

At about 4 p.m., after Donna had left for her nursing job, I went to the watchtower to observe this lady's activity.

Upon entering the room, she immediately turned on the television and departed for the bathroom to engage in noisy urination. She was a side-saddle sitter—in other words, sitting on the toilet sideways, or obliquely, in contrast to normal facing-the-front sitters.

Individuals vary in their approach to the toilet seat. Some sit with their backs against the water closet. Some lean forward. Some so far forward, that I have seen at least one individual fall on his face in the midst of having a bowel movement. The strangest approach was an individual who always sat facing the water closet with his legs straddling the commode. He was able to rest his arms on the water closet from that position. Several individuals have been observed to never sit down on the toilet, just assumed a sort of squatting position over the commode, possibly in order not to acquire any germs. Every imaginable position or approach to the commode has been observed.

After leaving the bathroom, the female subject undressed and exposed a beautiful body to the delighted eyes of the obsessive Voyeur. For the next hour and a half, this young female primped, adorned, arranged, and carefully dressed her hair, and was so finicky in her styling she could never quite get it correct. For the longest time, she took off and reinstalled a set of earrings and continued looking in admiration or condemnation at her image in the mirror.

Suddenly, she would smile at herself, and then appear disgusted at her appearance.

Finally, her husband joined her in the motel room, having come from his reserve meeting. They embraced and after discussing his reserve meeting, she became disturbed that he didn't notice her new earrings, and that she had gotten her ears pierced. During these disagreeable moments he accused her of unnecessarily spending money for getting her ears pierced and buying the earrings. She became upset and explained that this was one of the reasons why she accompanied him to Denver, to get her ears pierced and buy the earrings. They soon left for dinner, and after returning they appeared to have rectified their earlier disagreement. They turned on the TV, and she undressed quickly while he went to the bathroom. She pulled the straps of her bra down over her shoulders, and then placed a long thick nightgown over her head and pulled the bra out from underneath. She got in bed and pulled the covers up to her chin.

He came back and turned out all the lights and the TV, but left the bathroom door ajar, in which the light remained on. This afforded the opportunity to at least record some observation of this unhappy couple. After penetrating her without any foreplay or sufficient lubrication, he set the sex act in motion with vigorous thrusting and pulled the covers up to his neck so that no one could see his movements. She started complaining that he was hurting her, but he said, "You always say it hurts," and he continued his thrusting until his orgasm resulted in approximately five minutes. She got no satisfaction whatsoever. Soon she was again complaining about him not noticing or approving of her earrings.

Conclusion: This is real life. These are real people! I'm thoroughly disgusted that I alone must bear the burden of my observations. These subjects will never find happiness and divorce is inevitable. He doesn't know the first thing about sex or its application. The only thing he knows is penetration and thrusting, to orgasm, under the covers with the lights out.

My voyeurism has contributed immensely to my becoming a futilitarian, and I hate this conditioning of my soul. What is so distasteful is that the majority of subjects are in concert with these individuals in both design and plan. Many different approaches to life would be immediately implemented, if our society would have the opportunity to be Voyeur for a Day.

NINE

As GERALD Foos reflected on his "burden" as a committed voyeur, one who spent endless hours in solitude, linked primarily to the world below through the holes in his ceiling, he saw himself as an entrapped figure. He had no control over what he saw nor escape from its influence. His mood swings varied from day to day, hour to hour, guided by his guests.

Whether emotionally moved by the sight of a paralyzed veteran seeking sexual pleasure, or repulsed while watching the sidesaddle lady in bed with her boorish husband, Foos's words in his journal increasingly expressed feelings of dissatisfaction with his prolonged idling in the attic.

As I continued to read sections from his work ranging from the late 1960s into the mid-1970s, he appeared to be distancing himself from himself, changing from a first-person narrator to a character he wrote about in the third person. Sometimes he used the word "I," sometimes he referred to himself as "the Voyeur and Gerald," and at other times just "the Voyeur."

Watching the sunset descending over the Rocky Mountains is something of a ritual for the Voyeur and Gerald. The sun sinks slowly below the horizon draping the mountains in veils of orange and red.

With each sunset, it marks a new night of observation—as long as the guests in the rooms oblige. The Voyeur's nights on the observation platform begin well enough, but before long the Voyeur begins frowning at the non-action in the guest rooms . . . After a night of many observations, the Voyeur would climb down from the platform and watch the breaking of the dawn. He lived on simple food, and when weary he sat down and wrote in his journal, recording the happenings. The Voyeur thought of how excellent the morning air smelled, and made out-of-the-way excursions along the outside corridor of the motel, into which compartments or rooms open along the narrow passageway, to accomplish his mission of determining whether or not lights were on in the rooms that the Voyeur had just observed. He was always aware of the goings-on in his motel, and the rooms which housed the observable guests, and he paused and hoped to get a glimpse of a guest coming from a room which he had observed during the night, and have perhaps a small conversation . . .

And he sometimes believed he could communicate from the attic to his guests via mental telepathy.

For example, this particular evening the female subject was reclining on the bed, the television was off, and it was very quiet in the room below the vent. She was clearly of Scandinavian extraction, her hair being ash blonde, her eyes pale blue, her skin fair and freckled. Her figure was soft and supple, yielding and yearning. Her straight hair fell to just below her shoulders and was cropped in bangs across her forehead. Her mouth was full-lipped and the bright pink color of bubble gum. The same shade of pink color was evident under the bodice of her gauzy, silken nightgown, which peaked with her large, slightly pendulous breasts . . .

She lowered her right hand from her breasts to her vagina and began to rub her clitoris, seeming to be caught up in the rapture which was coursing through her body, and the clammy smell of the fragrant vaginal moisture grew stronger, more powerful to the observing Voyeur's nose only six feet away.

Then her restlessness disappeared as she reclined on the bed and began reading a book. Because it had been an incurious and uneventful day in the observation laboratory, the Voyeur decided to conduct an experiment utilizing the female subject. The Voyeur had been conducting this identical experiment during the past two years, and he has realized some success exploiting receptive-intelligent subjects.

The Voyeur began to concentrate on the female subject's eyes and attempt to transfer a thought. The thought the Voyeur was attempting to transfer was for the subject to raise her eyes from the book and look upward toward the vent. After several frustrating minutes of concentration, she finally raised her eyes and looked at the observation vent. Was this just an accident of voluntary movement, or had the Voyeur actually communicated

using brain waves? On several other occasions, the Voyeur en-
couraged a female subject to raise her eyes to the vent. This
particular female subject was definitely marked by extraordi-
nary perception. But after concentrating on the female subject
for some time, she apparently became uneasy with this unknown
phenomenon that was thrust upon her intellectuality and she
went to the bathroom and closed the door. The experiment ended
when she returned to the room, turned out the light and retired.

Conclusion: If the subject is a female, and has just concluded
masturbation, you have an excellent opportunity of getting her to
respond. This is perhaps because of her concentration level being
expanded. Female subjects appear to respond progressively better
to the Voyeur than male subjects. This is probably due to the fact
that the Voyeur's interest is primarily concerned with females, and
he experiences a stronger thought level in this application . . . The
Voyeur will continue with these experiments and will report any
significant discoveries to the journal in the future.

Often Foss would spend several stressful hours becoming ir-
ritated at watching people watching television—especially
those attractive couples who, instead of having sex, spent all
their time in bed arguing over what to watch, with the men
maintaining control over the clicker while the resentful women
eventually buried themselves under the blankets.

We have become a nation of TV maniacs, depending on this me-
dium to supply all our emotional needs. It is a rare occasion when
the TV isn't turned on.

Equally offensive were the heavy smokers, sending their toxins up through the vents for him to inhale; and there were also those guests bringing fast food into the rooms and then wiping off their greasy hands on the bed linen. Only once while posted in the attic, from which he witnessed the private behavior of close to three hundred guests per year, did he lose his concentration as a silent observer and actually speak through a vent to a person below.

The Voyeur passed No.6 vent and noticed this fastidious subject was eating Kentucky Fried Chicken while sitting on the bed. He had checked in earlier in the day and apparently was between appointments. The male subject was clean, seemingly of average intelligence, but clearly had messy and untidy eating habits. He had received napkins at the fast-food restaurant because they were positioned on the bed, but he made no use of them. Instead, he rubbed his hands on the bedspread, which was going to be difficult to clean.

The Voyeur continued his ocular inspection of this male subject expressing absolute disregard for the property of the motel, and the latter also began wiping his beard and mouth on the bedspread!

At this point, the Voyeur was in a state of frenzy, and in momentarily forgetting the precariousness of his position over the platform vent, he angrily shouted:

"You Son-Of-A-Bitch!"

The Voyeur immediately thought:

"Oh, God, did he hear me?"

The subject stopped eating and looked around the room, and then went to the window and looked outside. Apparently he knew someone had shouted S.O.B., but couldn't determine from which direction the insult came. He went to the window and looked out for the second time and pondered the situation for a few minutes, and then continued with his animalistic eating habits.

The Voyeur was relieved, and promised himself to maintain better control over his emotions in the future.

TEN

BUT FOOS would again lose control, and though he was aggravated once more by his guests' eating habits, the source of his provocation this time would be a frustration of his voyeuristic desire.

Donna checked into No. 4 this couple who were here on a cattle-buying trip. They were from Roundup, Montana, and the wife was a lovely and slender blonde of about twenty-five, while the husband was a little older, ruggedly handsome, and about 6 feet and 185 lbs. They checked in at approximately 5:30 p.m. and it was getting dark as I ascended to my observation laboratory to watch.

They had picked up hamburgers at McDonald's and began eating as soon as they entered. I immediately noticed that she was very beautiful, and had a fantastic figure. She was wearing boots, jeans, and a tight Western shirt, and it was well established that she was in the D-cup category.

But as I watch this young couple eat, it is obvious they had no manners. They just eat as fast as possible, dropping bits and pieces in their laps, and then brush it off onto the floor. Young people don't use napkins, at least the majority—just wipe their hands on their blue jeans or the bed sheets.

Oh, well, maybe I'll get to see some sex anyway.

They were both very non-communicative and he laid on the bed fully dressed and watched TV for the majority of the evening. She wrote a letter and departed to the bathroom and closed the door and remained for the better part of an hour.

When she came out, he crudely replied: "You stayed in there so long I'll bet you have a ring around your butt." This is the first thing he said all evening, typical cowboy talk. She was definitely embarrassed by this statement from this vulgar primitive idiot.

He continued watching a re-run of Gunsmoke and she went to the bathroom again. When she returned, she was wearing a nightgown with a robe over the top.

God, I'm never going to get to observe those magnificent breasts! These are the times it is difficult being a Voyeur, when your desire to observe is not being fulfilled. She sits on the chair and he smokes and watches TV, and not any word of communication results between them. What I am observing here is exactly what occurs in the relationship of about 90 percent of all couples.

Much later, he undressed and they go to bed. He is now feeling like sex, but she isn't, especially since he had insulted her earlier. When he removed his boots, I detected a smell that approached the vent that wasn't pleasant. He should have taken a shower if he *wanted to approach her, but he didn't. After fondling her through the nightgown and robe, he was making headway toward getting her aroused.*

By this time, I think maybe I'll get to observe those breasts yet, but no, he immediately gets out of bed and turns off the lights and the television!

Now I'm thoroughly mad and disgusted with the S.O.B. I feel like killing him. He now returns to the bed and begins his lovemaking in an atmosphere he is comfortable with: namely, darkness.

I won't stand for this at all. I return to the ground level and get in my car, and then drive it and park it directly in front of the #4 unit, parking it and leaving it there with the bright lights beaming on their window.

Returning to the observation platform, he is standing up peeking through the curtains, complaining that "some son-of-a-bitch has left his lights on."

In order to accomplish the remainder of his lovemaking procedure, he placates his position by getting under the covers to eliminate the light. He finally gets her undressed because I see her hands appear on the side of the bed dropping her robe and nightgown out. The room is lit up real well, and he begins his animal-like thrusting under the covers. He is finished in three minutes, and immediately withdraws and departs for the bathroom.

I finally get to see her body when she uncovers to wipe the semen away on my bedspread. She is very beautifully proportioned, but probably equally stupid and dumb.

He comes back from the bathroom and notes that the lights outside are still on. He says, "I wonder what the situation is with this car with the lights on."

Stupid bastard, he'll never know what my situation is, but I am well informed as to his unfortunate position in life.

Conclusion: I am still unable to determine what function I serve . . . Apparently, I'm delegated the responsibility of this heavy burden to be placed upon myself—never being able to tell anyone! If vanity or fate appoints this position for me in life, then I will be appreciably diminished by this unfair compromise. The depression builds, but I will continue onward with my research. I've pondered on occasion that perhaps I don't exist, only represent a product of the subjects' dreams. No one would believe my accomplishments as a Voyeur anyway, and therefore the dreamlike manifestation would explain my reality.

There is definitely a correlation between subjects who want the lights off during sexual activity and their profile. Normally, subjects from rural areas; non-educated types; minority groups; older generation subjects; southern-influenced subjects—are inclined to indulge in sex in darkness. After observing so many of these subjects, I can tell almost immediately the subjects who will turn the lights out. It is difficult to explain, but I accurately recorded an entire year of subjects who turned off the lights and those who left it on during sexual activity. Ninety percent of those who turned off the light fell within the category described above.

ELEVEN

THE LIMITED dimensions of the motel's room space, and the relatively short periods of time that existed between the entrances and exits of his guests—he rented Room 4 to five different "hot sheet" guests on one memorable New Year's Eve—meant that the larger lives of the Voyeur's subjects usually remained undetermined; but sometimes, if the guests who had drawn his special interest were also residents of the Denver area, he would capitalize on the convenience and stealthily visit their homes.

One woman he followed home was a middle-aged, overweight individual of close to fifty who had sex at the Manor House Motel one evening with a well-dressed and attractive gentleman in his early thirties.

From detailed conversation by the subjects, it was learned that they had met at a P.W.O.P. (Parents Without Partners) dance.

In the motel, after pouring and mixing a drink for the two of them, the female subject dropped her skirt to the floor and quickly pulled off her sweater. Then she said: "Undress me. Take off my bra and panties."

The male subject grasped the snap of her bra, and, in a flash, it was gone, and the female subject's full breasts jiggled, with the right one being one-third larger than the left, and they hung in a pendulous fashion.

"Do you like my body, darling?" she asked.

"It's fantastic," he said. "You're gorgeous."

The male subject didn't waste time. After removing her panties, he moved her to the bed and, after undressing himself, he moved down and touched his mouth on her vagina, and soon she was crying frantically, "Lick me, baby."

The male subject then withdrew his mouth and fingers and said, "I'm having difficulty making my car payment."

She moved away and reached toward the bed table for her purse, and gave him a hundred-dollar bill . . .

After fifteen minutes, the female subject had her orgasm, and she made an effort to perform fellatio on the male subject, but he said, "I'm really tired, but I need an extra fifty dollars to finish paying my bills." She again reached for her purse, paid him the money, and then she slid her mouth all the way down his penis— directly below the vent of the viewing Voyeur.

She took great interest in performing oral sex on him, and then completely engulfed his penis, extracting all the available semen he could produce.

The total act took fifteen minutes, and he was gone in his car. I wanted to know more about her, so I followed her to a retirement community near the motel. She went into an end unit of the complex and I waited for a few minutes for her to settle down. I approached her unit from the darkened side of the garage, and her back kitchen window had the curtain drawn open. Upon observation, I could see through the kitchen area into the living room and determined she lived alone with only a dog for companionship. She was walking around the living room area crying. She was in tears and appeared to be visibly upset.

I walked to the front and noticed her name on the mailbox as being the only person who lived there. I walked down the block, and inquired about her at an adjacent apartment, and was told her husband had been killed in Vietnam and her son was away, attending college.

Conclusion: The discovery of the tremendous sexual desire that some women of middle age express during these encounters is a definite tragedy. They have no sexual partners because they aren't attractive enough to acquire male partners, or they are reserved and hesitant. The gigolos, such as this particular one, promise elderly women sexual pleasure and social companionship. But I have seen this same gigolo in the motel with older men. He appears to be able to satisfy either women or men, and is quite unusual in demonstrating with ease this adjustment.

TWELVE

ANOTHER SUBJECT of interest to Gerald Foos was a fifty-year-old male physician who was affiliated with a different medical facility than Donna; and, presumably, the doctor had no idea that the motel he favored for his "hot sheet" midday interludes was co-owned by a nurse. Gerald Foos had observed him before, and was predisposed to dislike him, but then, Foos's instinctive feelings toward physicians were rarely positive.

Most doctors bear a mystique about themselves, as if they represent the hierarchy of mankind and everyone else should be subservient to their whims . . . Anyway, I assigned this particular doctor to Room 9, and, as I observed him from the platform, he entered the room alone, well-dressed and composed. He was about thirty-five, maybe 5 feet 9 inches and 150 lbs, close-trimmed dark hair. In the bathroom he loosened his tie and looked in the mirror,

*expressing what appeared to be much satisfaction with himself.
And then I saw him urinating in the sink! Yes, he definitely was
urinating in the sink! For what ungodly reason did he do that?
And then he washed his hands and the penis in the sink with his
trousers down to his knees.*

There was a knock on the door.

*He hurried to get his pants up, went to the door, and he let
in a lovely young woman who was wearing a nurse's uniform.
She was really beautiful. She is much better looking than the last
woman he brought to this motel. This woman embraced him but
was also very professional in conversation, discussing happenings
in the office and the status of certain patients.*

*She took off her uniform, went to the bathroom, and left the
door open. Imagine, this absolute feeling of freedom and openness.
Then she returned to the bedroom, standing directly beneath the
vent as he kissed her and removed a large beautiful breast from her
bra and sucked on it, gently teasing the nipple.*

*She responded by lowering the zipper of his pants and re-
moving his penis. She sat on the bed directly below, holding his
slow-rising penis in her hands and then kissing its red, purplish
head as he stood in front of her. He undressed while she continued to suck his penis, and then fell on the bed beside her and
undid her bra, releasing both of those magnificent breasts. The
areolas were dark and large, indicating she probably had children somewhere.*

*They assumed the 69 position, with her on top, and she con-
tinued this until she had an orgasm, and then another. She continued to suck on his penis, and then he came, too, after his toes had*

curled up and while he drove his fingers into her back. After she sucked from his penis the last dregs of his seminal fluid, he said, "My God, Darlene, you almost turned me inside out."

"I always love to swallow semen," she said. "I've always loved to feel a penis coming in my mouth."

They rested and then had three other sexual acts that afternoon—one of the most unbelievable pure sex exhibitions I have witnessed in years of observing.

After the doctor had left, and she was taking a shower, I decided I would follow her. I waited in my car, and then trailed her as she got into her station wagon and began a fifteen-minute drive that led us finally into a nice middle-class subdivision. As she turned into the driveway of a very nice house, I slowed down and parked along the street, watching her through my binoculars. There were tricycles on her lawn and a swing-set in the backyard. Then I noticed two small children running out to greet her as she climbed out of her car.

They went inside and I stayed there watching behind some hedges. It was getting dark. Soon another car pulled into her driveway. It was a man in a business suit. Probably her husband. I saw her meet him at the door with her arms outstretched and kiss him directly with the same lips that had so perfectly housed another man's penis only two hours before.

Conclusion: From the appearance of her career, her home, her children, and this presentable man, all the necessary ingredients for a successful marriage are on display. Maybe he neglects her. Maybe she just needs additional partners to satisfy her over-abundant sexual nature. I must keep watching.

Of the 296 sexually active guests that Gerald Foos watched and wrote about in an annual report on 1973, 195 were heterosexual white people who generally favored intercourse in the missionary position, and less frequently accompanied it with oral sex and masturbation. But regardless of these individuals' preferred positions or techniques in bed, the overall result produced an annual total of 184 male orgasms and thirty-three female orgasms—a figure that Foos conceded might be high, due to women's acting talents in faking orgasms in the interest of flattering their partners, or gaining quicker relief from their partners, or a bit of both.

In addition to the 195 heterosexual whites, the remaining seventy-four guests (within the total count of 296) were separately accounted for in Foos's journal as follows:

★There were twenty-six sexually active black heterosexual guests, and their preferred positions and orgasmic ratio was similar to the whites.

★There were ten white lesbian guests, all of whom Gerald Foos observed taking turns performing cunnilingus.

★There were seven white homosexual males exchanging oral and anal sex.

★There were ten guests who participated in interracial sex and who also engaged in oral sex and intercourse.

★There were fifteen registered guests (some alone, some with companions) whose sexual behavior, or asexual behavior, or aberrant behavior, or nondescript behavior was categorized within The Voyeur's Journal as part of a miscellaneous mélange; and, as examples, he presented three vignettes.

Vignette No. 1:

From the observation deck, I noticed all the regular activities usually associated with an afternoon sexual romp. He is kissing her and fondling her immediately below my position over the vent. After embracing for several minutes, they open a bottle of bourbon and pour themselves a drink, which is mixed with 7UP. The conversation narrows to a point concerning a dinner they enjoyed last week at the Top of the Rockies.

After this conversation, she excuses herself and goes to the bathroom and closes the door. Immediately he grabs her drink and takes his penis out of his pants and urinates in her drink. She came out of the bathroom and he said, "Here's to us," raising his glass and she obliged by taking her drink and drinking it. He was watching her carefully as she drank the urine-laden drink and he said, "This is really good bourbon, isn't it?"

She replied, "Yes, it is."

He said, "You ever tasted any better bourbon?"

She said, "In fact, I haven't."

He appeared to suddenly become very sexually aroused. Without another word, he leaned over and gave her a long, tongue-drenching kiss and she parted her lips and sucked on his tongue . . .

Conclusion: This male subject displayed an aberration which I had not observed in the past. The subject probably would also take an interest in watching a person urinate, being urinated upon, or urinating on someone else, if given the opportunity.

Vignette No. 2:

During the afternoon hours, the Voyeur checked in two neatly-dressed men from Florida and they were assigned to room No. 9. The Voyeur didn't observe the subjects during the evening because of disinterest. The next day the maid assigned to clean No. 9 came into the office and told me: "I think those two men have a sheep in there because I have heard lots of 'baa baas' and you should check it out."

The Voyeur proceeded to the observation platform and soon saw the older and heavier male sitting on the bed watching the younger male beginning to dress in a costume that appeared to be that of a goat with horns. The younger male placed the bedizenment of goat canonicals over his head like a tarpaulin. The bizarre garment was basically black in color and had a long white tail of perhaps two feet in length.

After the younger male completed dressing in this freakish costume, he immediately jumped to the floor on his hands and knees and began crawling and running around the motel floor. While he was demonstrating this ostentatious spectacle, he was vocalizing and uttering sounds similar to the cries of a distant sheep or goat.

The aberration continued until he had circled the motel room several times, when the rotund male subject proceeded to chase the younger male on hands and knees.

"You are heavenly," the rotund male said, "I have never seen a more beautiful sheep-boy."

Then the rotund man raised the long white tail with his hands and, with his erect penis, gouged through the young man's buttocks while the latter called out, "baa, baa." Later, the older man eased himself out of the younger man, and lay on top of him, holding him delicately, and then, after turning him over, began sucking his penis until orgasm . . .

Conclusion: This condition could perhaps be classified as a perversity, but it should not be condemned because both individuals are willing participants, and therefore the Voyeur will remain nondiscriminatory in its interpretation.

Vignette No. 3:

Checked in this handsome male into Room 6 and thought he would probably bring in a girl later. Upon observation, he brought a suitcase into the room, opened it, and placed it on the bed. Seeing that it contained only women's clothes, I immediately thought they probably were for a girlfriend that would visit him later.

He removed all his clothes and, after lining all the women's in a row on the bed, he picked up each article of clothing and gently fondled it and looked at it with great appreciation. He then appeared to attest to a sense of great pleasure and relaxation when viewing these clothes of the opposite sex, expressing a relish for the feel of the material.

After carefully dressing in this woman's attire, he was greatly impressed with his view in the mirror, and then sat down and applied substantial amounts of make-up to complete his cross-dressing.

After parading around the room for several minutes, he departed the room for destinations unknown to me. I did not see him return and he probably checked out that evening when he returned.

Conclusion: Transvestites or cross-dressing individuals have been observed on only two or three occasions. Therefore, I consider this to be a rare practice. This male was observed taking off a wedding band, and is probably married. He wanted a place to demonstrate his behavior and chose a motel where he would feel secure. This man's cross-dressing allowed him to express the gentle, graceful, sensuous side of his nature that society does not permit him to express as a man.

THIRTEEN

ACCORDING TO the Voyeur's report on 1974, which was his eighth annual summarization of what he saw and heard since he began watching people from his attic hideaway in 1966, there were 329 guests whose sexual activities he believed warranted attention and description in his journal. But much of what he saw in 1974 was similar to what he had seen in 1973, and in earlier years as well, except for two categories: oral sex among white heterosexual guests, which rose from only 12 percent to 44 percent, perhaps affected by the release of the pornographic film *Deep Throat* in the summer of 1972, and interracial sex.

During the entire year of 1973, he had observed only five interracial couples having sex, whereas in 1974 this number more than doubled to twelve couples; and it doubled again, between 1975 and 1980, to an average of twenty-five couples. He added, "The most amazing statistic is the almost complete participation in oral sexual adventures by interracial couples, which is practically total for both partners."

What was also a sign of change, beginning in the mid-1970s, was the casual manner in which interracial couples approached the front office while registering for rooms. A decade earlier, in the mid-1960s, the Voyeur noted that a white woman, for example, would never accompany her black lover while he registered. She would usually remain in the car, and join him later after he had obtained the key and occupied the room.

But by the mid-1970s such reticence on the part of either a white or black woman was replaced by the sight of couples standing together at the registration desk—which the Voyeur saw as one of many examples in which his small motel reflected the changing social trends and evolving attitudes that were spreading through the nation.

And, on a strictly personal note, the Voyeur acknowledged that he found watching interracial sex to be especially stimulating, and on one occasion it was the source of his most "explosive orgasm."

On the observation platform, on this autumn evening in 1976, the Voyeur is masturbating while watching a white woman almost choking because the black penis in her mouth is too large for her to contain. But she continues to give her partner fellatio, sucking his penis on one side and then the other, and suddenly, as he begins to come, she removes her mouth—and then she watches as this black man's sperm begins shooting up in the air about three or four feet

toward the observation vent. At the same time, the Voyeur in the
attic is also having an orgasm, right in tandem with the black
man. The Voyeur propels a strong first spasm of sperm right onto
the vent, and then it begins to drip downward to the foot of the
bed below.

   The woman, still grasping the end of the bed, sees evidence of
sperm spotting the bed cover. Then she looks up to see more sperm
dripping from the vent, and she says to her partner: "My gosh,
you shot your come right across the bed and up to the heating
vent!" She raised herself on the bed and wiped her finger across
the vent. She then placed her fingers in her mouth. "Yes," she said,
"this tastes like your come."

   And the Voyeur watched quietly as she proceeded to sample
his sperm.

As a footnote to this incident, the Voyeur asked in his journal, "Will anybody believe that this actually happened?"

If I had not seen the observation platform with my own eyes,
I would have found it hard to believe Foos's entire account.
Indeed, over the decades since we met, in 1980, I had noticed
various inconsistencies in his story: for instance, the first en-
tries in his Voyeur's Journal are dated 1966, but the deed of sale
for the Manor House, which I obtained recently from the Arapahoe County Clerk and Recorder's Office, shows that he purchased the place in 1969. And there are other dates in his notes
and journals that don't quite scan. I have no doubt that Foos
was an epic voyeur, but he could sometimes be an inaccurate

and unreliable narrator. I cannot vouch for every detail that he recounts in his manuscript.

By necessity, Foos existed in the shadows, doing so successfully for many years, a success he felt was worthy of note—while, at the same time, he had created a unique laboratory for the study of secret human behavior, for which he also believed he deserved some credit. As he saw it, he was not some lurid "Peeping Tom" but rather a pioneering researcher whose efforts were comparable to those of the renowned sexologists at the Kinsey Institute and the Masters & Johnson Institute. Much of the research and record-keeping at these places was obtained while observing volunteer participants, whereas his subjects never knew they were being watched and therefore he saw his findings as more representative of unconscious and unadulterated realism.

Gerald was not purely a removed observer, however. "In order to discover what individuals will do if provided with the proper sexual stimulation," the Voyeur planted "sexual paraphernalia and hard-core pornography in their rooms."

The Voyeur purchased fifty dildos and several hard-core pornographic magazines as an experiment. I would conceal one dildo and one pornographic magazine in a room, usually in the drawer of a nightstand, and then wait for an unsuspecting subject, and place her, or him, or a couple in that room, depending on what type of information was desired from the subject.

During this period of observation, the Voyeur didn't have any of the individuals complain or return any of the planted sexual paraphernalia. Fifty percent of the women utilized the dildo or magazines, the other fifty percent either ignored the devices or discarded them.

One of those 50 percent who utilized the planted materials was a nun.

In his journal, Gerald wrote that his experimentation and observation had a higher purpose.

"The only way that our society is going to achieve proper sexual stability and mental health, which are undisputed requirements for maturity, is to know the truth of what people are actually doing in the privacy of their own bedrooms. We must educate people with the truth, not indoctrinate; teach facts, not fallacies; formulate a code that accepts all sexual practices, not preaches asceticism."

While it was true that Donna was fully aware of his activities, and on occasion joined him in the attic as a second witness and sexual partner, he nevertheless felt a need for wider recognition. He admitted as much in his writing, which during the mid-1970s began to reflect, not only what he saw and felt while watching other people, but also how he saw and felt about himself, beginning with his origins as a farm boy whose infatuation with his beautiful aunt Katheryn led him into a lifetime of voyeurism.

In his written account, he described how he used to sneak out of his bedroom at night and slowly make his way along a dirt road to crouch below her lighted window in anticipation of seeing her nude. Describing himself in the third person, as he did in much of his writing:

The youth moved silently through the night over the grass and across the barbed wire fence . . . her shutters folded back, unsuspecting, letting the northwest breeze play through the arrangement of the bedroom. The youth looked in, forgot about the cold and rain outside, forgot about essence, forgot about time. While observing his aunt she began to move toward her collectables, which were small miniature dolls and thimbles which were encased in a wooden receptacle on her wall. My aunt was naked as she moved toward her collections very cautiously, and began to handle the thimbles prudently and discreetly. Her actions in handling the thimbles and miniature dolls were accomplished in a cavalier manner, bringing them close to her naked breasts in a sort of sexual ritual not understood by the observing youth.

He also could not understand why his aunt Katheryn was so different from his modest mother and the rest of the family, in neglecting to wear a robe or nightgown while walking around in her bedroom with the shutters folded back. But he could no more ask questions about this than he could explain his own behavior and the punishment he risked should his prowling become known to his aunt or another family member who happened to see him near her window at night.

The closest he came to admitting his special interest in her occurred one day when he confessed to his mother, prior to his tenth birthday, that he was envious of his aunt's thimble and doll collection and wanted a collection of his own. (He had already stolen one of his aunt's thimbles while she was away on a short vacation, but he returned it in time to avoid being reprimanded).

"Well, you can't collect dolls," his mother said, "but why don't you begin collecting sports cards?" She added, "When I'm at Gambles Hardware, I'll buy you a couple of packs."

This started him off on a lifelong hobby with sports cards, one in which he would amass tens of thousands of sports cards by the time I met him in 1980, when he was forty-five, and in his fifteenth year at the Manor House Motel. But his collecting was always associated with his boyhood attraction to his aunt Katheryn, as he explained in his notes.

> *The youth will confuse sexuality and the art of accumulating objects . . . there was a direct association from his aunt being nude and [his] collecting. Because his tenth birthday was days away, he vowed to begin a collecting routine almost immediately in order to imitate the actions of his aunt.*

But even before he was ten, his aunt's presence induced early signs of his foot fetish that he later imposed on his high school girlfriend, Barbara White, leading to the couple's breakup. "My aunt would come over for coffee in the morning to see my mom. I was six or so, under the table, looking at my aunt Katheryn's feet. She wore open-toed shoes. I wanted to touch her toes."

In addition to collecting cards—in later years he would also collect stamps, coins, and vintage firearms—he had a boyhood interest in muskrat tails.

> *I collected muskrat tails to determine which was the longest or the shortest. This endeavor was abundantly available to me, because*

my father was a trapper of muskrats to supplement the family income in the winter months. I was delegated the duty to feed the skinned muskrats to the hogs, and that is when I noticed that muskrats did not have an even length of tails. After a few weeks, I would tire of one particular length and shape, and then after collecting the tail of choice, I would begin the process again, keeping the other tails in a can. I did this unscrupulously and finally my parents objected to the special odor in my room, and I was forbidden to collect muskrat tails. My sports card collecting, however, by comparison was a reasonable and respectable thing to be collecting. Without distinct knowledge, I was following a pattern laid down over time, which was the natural, predictable and aesthetically correct way of accumulating anything interesting.

While his habit of masturbating introduced him for the first time to physical pleasure, it was also accompanied by so much guilt that he sought moral guidance from a priest. "I went to an old and very strict priest for confession, and I asked him about it. To my surprise, he said it was not a sin. He said that every man and woman probably masturbated. He was not liberal in his beliefs, but he was compassionate toward me."

Gerald was also pleased to learn from an older classmate that no physical harm would result from the act of masturbating, and furthermore was told not to worry if he ever ejaculated a profusion of seminal fluid. "This older male confirmed to me that it was proper, it was OK—and that after I could shoot nine big drops, I'd be a man. Wow! I kept counting the volume and drops after receiving that advice, and finally it materialized."

FOURTEEN

GERALD WAS the first of two children born to Natalie and Jake Foos. Gerald was five years older than his brother, Jack, and while they were similarly reared, attended the same schools, and bore a physical resemblance—dark hair, dark eyes, pale coloring, big-boned, and tall—their difference in age and personality contributed to their not knowing one another very well. They had neither a rivalry nor a fraternal bond. In school they were never classmates, teammates, or confidants. Quietly, they went their own way. It was as if each were an only child.

Gerald was by nature a "loner," as he acknowledged in his writing. When he was not busy with farm chores, or spying on his aunt, or collecting cards, or riding his horse to grade school each morning, he would often "look up at the sky and know there was something out there for me." He sometimes carried a juvenile novel about the Wild West, or Mark Twain's *Adventures of Huckleberry Finn*, which he had borrowed from the town library. His mother had encouraged him to join the library, and while he sat at one of the tables he would glance up at the cases and see hundreds of books with brightly colored spines.

> *This was an astonishing sight to a boy who lived in a farm house where books are almost unknown . . . in a rural community lacking a common culture or aesthetic tradition, in the aftermath of the Great Depression in which people like my family and relatives worked, and worked, and had little time for reading more than newspapers . . . I was mesmerized by books, and what might be called "the life of the mind," and the life that was not manual labor, or farming, or housework, but seemed in its specialness to transcend these activities.*

The fact that Gerald had a younger brother was rarely referred to in his writing—except for one occasion when his parents asked that he share his bicycle with Jack, which he did willingly, and on another occasion when Gerald described the two of them standing in proximity to one another outside the house while their father, a onetime semipro baseball player, was trying to teach Gerald how to bunt.

> *My father's arms are around me. His hands are covering my hands, gently pushing them upward on my sturdy Louisville Slugger baseball bat. "You've got to choke up," dad tells me. "The bunt is all about control." My brother is mowing the front lawn, and he doesn't pay any attention to dad and me. "A bunt," dad says, "is a thing of beauty, an opportunity of something good to occur in the future."*

Maybe he focused exclusively on bunting because we couldn't hit away in the small backyard of that little house. I think it was more than that, though. The bunt isn't a game changer, like a home run or a triple. Instead it nudges things along, and keeps the ball as far as possible from where the opponents want it to be, a strategy, brains over brawn, and something my smart dad understood.

My brother and I haven't grown up to be Major League long ball hitters. Neither of us has changed the world. In the past few years, we've lost jobs, lost our swings, lost our confidence, lost our faith, lost dad. But thanks to him, we are masters of making do, stretching things out, getting the most from what opportunity offers. At keeping it going with nothing more than grit in our hearts, and our grip on the bat, ready for the bunt, that dad taught us.

Gerald and his brother Jack were both excellent all-around high school athletes, with Gerald being better in baseball, football, and track, and Jack (two inches taller than his six-foot older brother) superior at basketball and he was also one of the best discus throwers in the state.

During the four years that Gerald was away in the Navy, Jack was in high school. After Gerald's discharge, his marriage to Donna, and his buying the Manor House Motel, his brother was courting a young Colorado woman he had met in college and, after their marriage, the couple moved to Texas. Jack and his wife taught school there for a while, had children, eventually prospered in the real estate business, and became members of the Jehovah's Witnesses. Their devotedly Catholic mother, Natalie, was mortified by the news. As she expressed it to Gerald, "Your brother Jack is lost."

Neither she nor the rest of her family and kinfolk saw much of Jack after his conversion, but this was of no concern to Gerald. He was absorbed by his own interests and his private life in the attic. When he was not escorting Donna and their two young children for weekend visits to see his parents in the farming community, he was often writing about them and his years growing up with them—doing so while reclining on the attic's rug with his notebook, his pencil, and a flashlight. This became his regular routine: if he was bored with what he was seeing through the vents—if he was spending hours watching people watching television—he would shift his attentions from voyeurism to his personal history, where he would recall his boyhood adventures in rural Ault and his sorrows during a period of time he never seemed to outgrow.

The town was truly a rural paradise, surrounded by 2,000 neatly self-sufficient farms that survived the Depression and two World Wars, and the community was energized by the ranchers and farmers who kept Main Street alive. Here everyone knew everyone, and everyone's story was known. There were churches of every Protestant denomination, and one Catholic parish. Parades were held on Veteran's Day, Memorial Day, July 4, and a week in the middle of January was devoted to the Lamb Feeders Festival. The populace lined up on the main thoroughfare to watch the parades, floats, and home-crowned royalty.

The town's everyday royalty were its doctors and dentists, its high school teachers, and the football coach who'd taken the team to the state championships four times in a decade. The town doctors were especially respected and revered, and they still made house calls. The long dark hallway to our doctor's office on Main Street led steeply upstairs and the black rubber treads on the steps absorbed all sound. The doctor was tall, bald, and sardonic, and he could produce dimes from behind the necks and ears of his young patients, unfurling his closed hand to reveal the sparkle of a coin.

Following our appointment we'd drive five miles back to the farm, passing the fairgrounds and field, and the dome of the courthouse glowed gold. The hill behind the courthouse was lined with tall trees whose dense, leafy branches met over the street, and the branches appeared to lift as the cars passed. Open fields bordered our farm house, tasseled corn filled them in summer, and thick stalks of freshly mowed hay purified the air in the countryside with the most pleasing smell of all time. Cows grazed the high-banked meadow across the road and glanced over at us placidly. They sometimes spooked and ran off like clumsy girls, rolling their eyes and lolloping out of sight.

The telephone numbers in our town went from 3 to 5 digits. Ours was 13372. Aunt Katheryn's 227R2. My mother's car was a two-toned 1946 black Mercury sedan. The car was black and white, and flat as a boat. As we arrived home, my father would be cooking home-grown russet fried potatoes in the kitchen, "starting supper," the only domestic chore he ever performed. I knew he'd learned to peel potatoes in the Army, cutting those peels in one continuous spiral motion.

My dad, who was past thirty when he entered the Army, met my mother at a Lamb Feeders dance in 1933. He was 26. She was 19. He was handsome, a farmer, and had a car, a 1930 Ford. They

married in 1934, the year I was born. In the winter of 1940, when
my mother had two children, she was ill and undernourished, retired
to bed, and our doctor came to see her. She was now down to nearly
100 pounds. The doctor sat down beside her bed, his black bag on
the floor. "Now, Natalie," he said, while lighting two cigarettes,
"we're going to smoke this last one together."

His mother resisted cigarettes, regained her health, and
Gerald's life returned to normal. When he was not helping with
farm chores, or attending school, he was wandering around
town alone, feeling:

invisible, beneath the radar of adult supervision. The consequence
of so much unsupervised freedom was that I became precociously
independent. I don't mean that my parents didn't love me, or were
negligent in any way, but only that in the 1940s in this part of
the country there was not much awareness of danger. It wasn't un-
common that adolescent boys and girls hitchhiked on roads around
the region. I was allowed to see movies alone at the Prince Theater,
which was one of those ornate, elegantly decorated dream-palaces
first built in the 1920s. In the shadowy opulence of the Prince,
as in an unpredictably unfolding dream, I fell under the spell of
movies as I had fallen under the spell of books earlier. These serials
could be attended for ten cents, but you had to come back the next
Saturday to find out what happened.

Even on weekends the roads were relatively free of motorists,
and one day in 1947, when I was twelve, and skipping stones while
walking in the middle of a street, a beautiful flat stone I was

skipping took a high hop and went right through the first-floor window of Mr. Thomas's home.

My heart froze, and everything inside me screamed: "Run!"

But I didn't. I just stood there, not knowing what to do. Then I went up to Mr. Thomas's front door and knocked. A man's voice hollered: "Hold on!" I could hear somebody coming down the stairs. Then, after what seemed like an eternity, the door opened, and there stood Mr. Thomas.

Mr. Thomas was an elderly man, small and slender, and he raised chickens in his backyard, and had a reputation of not being too friendly. He looked at me and said: "What do you want?"

Now at this moment, I felt I'd made a mistake and I wished I'd run when I had a chance. But it was too late now. So I blurted out: "I was skipping stones, and by accident one hopped across the street and through your window, Mr. Thomas." By the time I told him everything, I'd nearly fainted from not breathing. Mr. Thomas leaned out around the door and looked at the window.

"You got any money to pay for it?"

I told him I didn't, and asked how much he thought it would cost.

"It'd run about $1.50 for the glass," he said, "and then, of course, I'll have to fix the window. What's your name, boy?"

"I'm Gerald Foos."

"Well, ask your mother if you can carry water for my chickens after school. If she says yes, I'll pay you a dollar a week, and you come here every day after school and Saturday mornings. After you pay for the window, you'll make some money for yourself. How's that sound?"

"Sounds fine, Mr. Thomas. I'll be here, right after school."

That was the beginning of one of my best memories. When I left Mr. Thomas, I felt super. I had done the right thing, and it turned out fine. Best of all, I felt I had learned the art of being brave and honest. It just wasn't talking to friends about being brave—no, this was the real thing, how I wanted to run but didn't.

When I told my mother I was making a dollar a week, she said, "As soon as you pay for that window, you can begin giving fifty cents a week for the house, and keep fifty cents for yourself, and no more skipping stones down the street."

So every day after school, and on Saturday mornings, I would lug water for the chickens. He had about two hundred. There were eight watering stations scattered throughout the chicken yard, and I had to carry eighteen buckets of water from the house, about 200 feet away, to get the job completed. The whole thing took me about an hour and a half, and I figured that six days times ninety minutes at one dollar a week came out to about eleven cents an hour, which is about what people earned at that time.

Mr. Thomas was my first adult friend, and he told me chickens are pretty stupid birds. He said, "You can go into the same chicken coup a hundred times, and those birds won't so much as ruffle a feather, but walk in there wearing a new pair of shoes, or a different hat, and they'll panic and fly all over the place."

I kept quiet, but I didn't think chickens were all that stupid. It's just that they don't like surprises. They feel safe with things they know. That's really not all that different from a lot of people I know, even if they are peculiar and funny looking.

FIFTEEN

To READ from Gerald Foos's journal is to learn that his first love in high school was the one lasting love of his lifetime, and to realize that, as a middle-aged man in the attic, he was nostalgic for when people used to watch *him* and cheered from the grandstands after he had hit a home run or scored a touchdown—and then, after the game, he would wait on the field for the arrival of his sweetheart, the star cheerleader, who would leap high in the air with her legs spread wide before landing lightly in his lap, her legs wrapped around him, and her arms embracing him in a way he would never forget.

This was in 1953, his senior year, and the local paper regularly printed his picture and described his achievements: ". . . Foos made a beautiful run, escaping a couple of potential tacklers at the line of scrimmage and plowing on after being hit again at the 10 . . ." He scored several touchdowns that year, and soon after Barbara White would be flying into his arms.

Twenty years later, after they were both married to others, and she had moved with her husband to Arizona, Gerald on impulse would sometimes leave the motel and drive alone eighty miles to his hometown. He would tell his wife that he was visiting his mother, Natalie, but he was really visiting the house where Barbara White used to live, and where during late winter afternoons she would smile down at him and, with an outstretched finger, print his name on the misty pane of her bedroom window.

She was the prettiest girl I'd ever seen, and also the nicest, because everyone liked her. I had first met her on a blind date arranged by one of her girlfriends, and I forgot about my apprehensions because I always wanted to date Barbara. Her smile greeted me cheerily, and the movie was fine, although I can't remember what we saw. What I do remember is during the movie I got my arm around her sheepishly, and that we kissed coming home in the car.

From that first time onward, we went steady for the next two years. We never did anything except hugging and kissing—which in those days, in the early 1950s, was one of the greatest things that ever occurred. Some of the young people who just have sex nowadays don't know what that feeling is, the feeling of having someone you really love and care about and the only thing you ever do is kiss them. I never had any intention of having sex with Barbara. The only thing I ever did, which broke us up, was the one time I wanted to see her feet.

We were parked behind the pump that pumps the water for the city of Ault. In those days many of the girls in school wore shoes that had the colors of the football team, which were black and red, and on this night Barbara's shoes were red and were illuminated from the light coming down from the pump house. As I looked at her shoes I think I was having a transfixed flow back to the toes of my aunt Katheryn, and, almost without thinking, I just reached down—schump!—and took off her shoe!

She said: "Gerald, what did you do that for?"

"Oh, I just wanted to see it, and wanted to do it."

"Don't do that again," she said.

So I lay the shoe down under her, on the floor of the truck, and we went back to kissing and necking. It was about midnight, or past. And then I saw her stocking foot, and I just thought I wanted to see her entire foot—and just went down and—scoop!— I took the stocking off as quick as I could.

Oh, she came apart on that! She was angry, and upset, and felt violated. And I had, of course, violated her trust, because I had never before touched any other part of her body except her back, and a shoulder, or arms. I never touched her legs, any place like that, because that was a taboo area, you just didn't do that, at least from my perspective, in the way I felt in those days. And so, consequently, Barbara immediately jumped out of the truck, stood there, and, while turning around, she pulled off the chain around her neck that had my ring, and she just threw it at the seat.

"I don't like it, Gerald," she said, and then she walked away, limping on one foot.

So I backed the truck out and pulled it over beside her, and I called out to her: "Hey, Barb, get in here. Quit acting like a dummy," or something like that. "These people out here will see us and think we're fighting."

"Don't you think we're fighting?"

"Oh come on, Barb, get in the truck. I'm sorry, I'm sorry, okay? You're my girl . . . just get in the truck, and let's talk about it."

She just kept on walking. Her house was only a block away. And so she limped all the way home.

Even many years later, years after I'd last seen her, if anyone mentioned her name, I'd fall to pieces. And whenever I drove past the house where she used to live—even if my car radio wasn't on—I'd hear the voice of Ray Charles singing:

> I can't stop loving you
>> I've made up my mind
>>> To live in memory
>>>> Of the lonesome times . . .

SIXTEEN

GERALD FOOS'S years in the Navy produced few insights or observations in his writing because, as he later explained to me, his most interesting experiences during this period were "top secret." After basic training and a tour in Hawaii—a photograph of Foos on the Waikiki Beach shows a spectacularly muscled young man posing bare chested in a bathing suit—he was selected to serve with underwater demolition teams, forerunners of the SEALs. While the Korean War had ended in 1953, he and his fellow crewmen maintained around-the-clock vigilance throughout the next four years while attached to a cruiser named the USS *Worcester*.

The ship had been in the Yellow Sea early in the war to assist in amphibious assaults on the North Korean military; but by the time Foos arrived, it had been reassigned to NATO operations in the Mediterranean. On some occasions it was diverted to the Atlantic Ocean with stopovers in such cities as Bar

Harbor, Boston, New York, and Norfolk before heading down to Guantanamo and Panama. Although his notes are brief on this subject, he acknowledged losing his virginity thanks to the hospitality of one particular bordello shaded by palm trees at some undisclosed location.

At sea with him always were erotic images of his aunt Katheryn and lasting recollections of his losing Barbara White. His voyeuristic passions subsided during his service years, diminished by the fear of being discovered and the disgrace he assumed would cling to him if he were dishonorably discharged. He made very few friends while in the Navy and corresponded mainly with his parents. His father, Jake, took care of the sports-card and memorabilia collection in Gerald's absence, and even added to it by acquiring such valuable items as a baseball signed by the Hall of Fame baseball player Honus Wagner, who was with the Pittsburgh Pirates in the early 1900s. Gerald wrote, "My father and I had very little in common except for our love of sports."

Jake Foos had been such a fine semipro baseball player in the early 1930s that a major league scout had expressed interest in signing him to a contract. Gerald had been told this by his mother, Natalie, who used to watch Jake play shortstop (Honus Wagner's position) for her hometown team, the Windsor Merchants, located in a wheat farming district in northern Colorado not far from Ault.

The Windsor Merchants were excellent, Natalie said, talented enough to have once defeated Leroy "Satchel" Paige's

African American barnstorming group that visited Windsor during the summer of 1934. Days earlier, Satchel Paige had been the winning pitcher at an annual tournament in Denver sponsored by the *Denver Post*, one that featured semipro and independent professional teams from around the nation and was including black players for the first time—this being thirteen years before Jackie Robinson would be admitted into the major leagues by the Brooklyn Dodgers, in 1947. (A year later, Satchel Paige came to the majors via the Cleveland Indians, at the age of forty-two.)

But Jake Foos (who, according to Natalie, singled twice against Paige during the exhibition game in Windsor) never aspired to being in the major leagues. In 1934 he had just gotten married and was about to have his first son; and, as Gerald described in his writing:

> *On the farm, Dad seemed happy just getting up early in the morning to be outdoors . . . In early spring we planted oats, wheat, corn, beets and beans, and milked the cows . . . At home, however, things weren't always peaceful. My Dad was a wonderful man and provider—until he drank. I knew the moment the ice cubes went into the glass, he would become a different person, an angry drunk. It was confusing to me, because sober he was very lovable. I didn't understand that Dad was an alcoholic, but just about everyone's father was in our part of the country, and that was especially true of Aunt Katheryn's husband, my uncle Charley.*

During one of Gerald Foos's furloughs while in the Navy, the USS *Worcester* remained at port in New York for a few days prior to leaving for Panama. After buying a ticket to a game at Yankee Stadium, Foos sat in the front row of the bleachers and had a close view of Mickey Mantle's back while the latter was standing in center field. Although Mantle hit a home run that day, Gerald was most impressed with Mantle's speed and agility while covering the outfield.

> *I watched Mickey Mantle take off after a long fly ball in the vast plain of centerfield, and I thought he wasn't going to catch it. I thought he wasn't running fast enough. He just seemed to be gliding easily beneath a speeding white speck, which he had detected before I heard the crack of the bat, and before I understood why Mantle was moving. And just as I was about to go insane worrying that Mantle wouldn't catch it, he let the ball sink into his glove as if he had known all along that his glove was the only place the ball wanted to go.*

In later years, Foos would collect many items relating to Mantle: vintage baseball cards, signed baseballs, a signed Louisville Slugger bat.

Years after being discharged, and many months after building the viewing platform in his attic, Gerald Foos felt at times that he was still in the Navy, adrift in calm waters, peering down through the louvered slats in his motel as he used to squint through his binoculars while on deck duty, directing his gaze outward for great distances without spotting anything of interest. His life in the attic was humdrum and uneventful. His motel was a dry-docked boat whose guests endlessly watched television, exchanged banalities, had sex mainly under the covers if they had sex at all, and gave him so little to write about that sometimes he wrote nothing at all.

Ordinary life is boring, he concluded, not for the first time; no wonder there is always a big market for make believe: staged dramas, films, works of fiction, and also the legalized mayhem inherent in such sports as boxing, hockey, and football. Gerald wrote, "Talking about football or hockey, if the players were armed with knives and guns, there would not be stadiums large enough to hold the crowds."

Gerald often witnessed examples of his guests' dishonesty, their admissions of double-dealing in their businesses, and their willingness to compromise their principles if it was financially profitable. They sometimes tried to cheat him out of the room rent, and hardly a week passed without him witnessing instances of chicanery whenever a male guest, eager for sex, entered the motel with a woman he did not know well. As described in The Voyeur's Journal:

> Checked in this "hot sheet" white male and white female in Room 9. He was a white-collar type in his 40s, 5'10", 175 lbs, average appearance; she was in mid-20s, 5'3", attractive.
>
> After they entered the room, the male immediately began negotiating a contract for sexual pleasure. He had offered her $25 for

oral sex and intercourse, but she said, "Give me $45 and I'll give you the best blowjob you've ever received. I'm an expert."

He finally agreed, and gave her the money.

"Take off your clothes and get comfortable," she said. After he had taken off his clothes, she said: "I need a Coca-Cola to keep my throat clear when I'm performing. Do you have any change for the machine?"

"I'll get the Coke for you," he said; but she said: "Oh, no, you're already undressed. I'll get it and be right back."

She took his change and left the room. As she was gone he began playing with his penis, attempting to get an erection. About ten minutes passed, and he was still waiting and playing with himself.

Finally, he got up, looked through the window, and said: "Son of a bitch—that whore's gone!"

He put on his clothes quickly and left the motel room. I immediately came down from the observation platform to see what was happening. But I missed seeing him go, and so I went to the office.

About fifteen minutes later, I see him heading back to Room 9. Returning to the observation platform, I see him taking off his clothes again, looking thoroughly disgusted. He now had a pornographic magazine, and was reclining on the bed, and then he began masturbating and finally ejaculated onto the centerfold photo of a nude model. He then ripped the photo out of the magazine and flushed it down the toilet.

Conclusion: Unfortunately for him, the woman he was with was not a prostitute but merely a con artist. Prostitutes rarely, if ever, operate using these con-game tactics. I have seen many hookers operate with their clients, and they are nearly always fair, and deliver whatever has been agreed upon. He should have recognized this woman's motive after she'd taken his forty-five bucks and then left him alone in the room with the excuse she was going out for a Coke.

SEVENTEEN

W RITTEN OVER so many years, Gerald's journal not only illuminates changing social patterns as seen through the observation vents, it reflects demographic changes as well. From 1960 to 1980, Colorado's population grew by 65 percent, over a million new residents, some of whom passed through the Manor House Motel. They were not always appreciated.

White working-class couple in their 30s, with a U-haul trailer attached to their old sedan, arrived from Chicago and rented a room for a week. He was a 6-foot man of about 190 lbs, and she was about 5'8", slim and of average appearance. Both were very talkative, and he in particular expressed a desire to acquire work in the area and ultimately settle here.

I observed them from time to time during the week and they were having a terrible time finding work and housing. Their sex life was non-existent, and when he would approach her she would resist him and also say something critical. She said he was not trying hard enough to get a job.

From time to time, he would discuss his problems with me in the office. But he would present a different attitude than the real one of desperation that I overheard from the vent. He told me that things were looking up. At the end of the week, when the room rent was due, he asked for a three-day extension, saying he was expecting a check from Chicago. I sympathized with his situation and granted his request.

During observation the next day, I overheard the guy telling his wife: "The dumb guy in the office thinks I have a check coming in from Chicago, and we'll fool him the same way we did at the motel in Omaha."

She was upset with him, saying he should get a job and stop taking advantage of people's generosity.

And so the bastard was a liar, and I decided to protect my interests and put a lock-out cover on their door knob. This device prevents a guest from getting their key to open the door. When the couple returned to their room, the guy comes rushing into the office, saying to me: "You told me we could stay until I received my check." I replied, "I've decided you should make other arrangements and pay for the room now." He said, "You know the check is coming in." "There's no guarantee," I said, and I went on to tell him I would retain his belongings until he pays for the room in full.

He angrily left. I waited for a half-hour and then changed the locks on his door and moved their belongings into our storage room.

Conclusion: Thousands of unhappy, discontented people are moving to Colorado in order to fulfill that deep yearning in their soul, hoping to improve their way of life, and arrive here without any money and discover only despair. . . . Society has taught us to lie, steal, and cheat, and deception is the paramount prerequisite in man's makeup. . . . As my observation of people approaches the fifth year, I am beginning to become pessimistic as to the direction our society is heading, and feel myself becoming more depressed as I determine the futility of it all.

In fact, I have recently created an honesty test, one in which I've placed some of our guests in a tempting situation. The first guest I tested was a U.S. Army lieutenant colonel in his mid-50s, who was just assigned to an administrative position at the Fitzsimons Army Hospital, and for a while he stayed in our motel's Room 10.

Foos explained the test briefly:

I begin by placing a small suitcase in the closet of Room 10. The suitcase is secured with a small inexpensive padlock that can easily be broken off, or pried loose, by almost any individual. Guests are always leaving behind small suitcases, and I use these for my experiment.

Whenever a guest that I want to test for honesty arrives at the motel, I book them in Room 10. Then, while they're filling out the registration form, I'll have my wife Donna telephone me from our living quarters, pretending she had been a guest and had left her suitcase in the room with $1,000 deposited inside.

"You say you left a suitcase containing $1,000?" I'll repeat to Donna aloud on the phone, assuming that the newly-arrived

guest at the desk is listening. Then I put down the phone and call back to my wife in the apartment: "Donna, did the maid turn in a small suitcase that somebody left with money inside?"

And Donna yells back: "No, she didn't. Nothing was found."

I would then pick up the phone and say to Donna on the line: "I'm sorry, sir, nothing has been found, but if it is, since we have your address, we'll send it to you promptly."

On this particular day, I conducted this fictitious exchange while the Army colonel is checking in. After he had filled out the form, I assign him to Room 10, and then I go up to the observation platform to watch what he does.

The first thing he does after entering the room is to place his luggage on the bed and he goes to the bathroom. When he comes out, he turns on the TV and quickly scouts the room. He reads the room-rate chart on the door. He opens and closes the bureau drawers. He removes his military jacket and hangs it in the closet. That's when he sees, resting on the closet shelf, the small suitcase. He takes it down and places it on the bed. He touches its small lock but doesn't try to open it. Like all the other guests in this situation, he momentarily ponders the situation.

This is the moment that I love to witness. The moment of truth or dishonesty is flashing through the person's mind. There is the question: Should I break open the lock and take the $1,000? Or should I be a Good Samaritan and turn it into the office? You can almost hear each person thinking to themselves: Nobody knows this suitcase is in this room, and there's $1,000 inside, and Lord knows I can use the money.

This particular Army colonel took ten minutes in coming to a decision. Finally, evil ultimately triumphed. He tried to twist off the lock with his fingers, but was unsuccessful. He departed the room, carefully closing the door, and returned with a screwdriver from his car. When he returned he was hesitant to use it. He left the room again and wandered into the office, where Donna saw him and said hello. He idled there for a few moments, as if considering whether anybody was on to the fact that he'd found the suitcase.

Then he returned to Room 10. He chain-locked the door, sat on the bed, and, with one motion with the screwdriver, he snapped open the suitcase. He began shuffling through the clothes packed in there, searching every crevice and every pocket. Suddenly, it dawned on him that there was no money in the suitcase, only clothing. He shook his head, indicating confusion and concern. Now what? He was probably thinking: I can't carry this suitcase to the office with the lock broken, and I can't just leave it in the room, either.

After another few minutes of pacing the room, the colonel reached for his raincoat, wrapped it around the suitcase, and departed from Room 10. I heard him start up his car, and then he apparently drove away to find a place where he could dispose of the suitcase.

The Voyeur in the observation tower reached for his notebook and recorded another example of a motel guest's greed.

Conclusion: After subjecting fifteen registered guests to this test—a number that included a minister, a lawyer, a few businessmen, a couple of working people, a vacationing couple, a middle-class married woman, and one man who was unemployed—only two of the entire list returned the suitcase to the office unopened. One was a doctor. The other was the middle-class married woman.

The minister and the others all opened the suitcase and then tried to dispose of it in different ways. The minister pushed the suitcase out of the bathroom window and tossed it into the hedges. The doctor, in fact, made an attempt to open it, but then changed his mind. And so of the fifteen test cases, only the woman was not tempted by greed.

The Voyeur rests his case.

EIGHTEEN

IN THE Voyeur's category of "honest, but unhappy people,"
a great majority of his subjects were out-of-town married couples who, during their brief stay at the Manor House Motel, so
filled his ears with their complaints or indications of long-term
marital stress that he constantly reminded himself of how
lucky he was to have Donna as a wife.

"Without her understanding and unprejudiced attitude,
my observation laboratory would never have become a reality.
My wife," Gerald wrote, made "every effort to understand the
motivations behind" his voyeurism. She "has not criticized or
condemned me for this perversion. Thus has she helped ratio-
nalize my conviction that voyeurism is a natural state of being,
and this desire is present in all men."

In her pretty and perky blonde embodiment he had an ador-
ing and faithful spouse, an in-house nurse, a coconspirator with
regard to his prying propensities, a prurient presence in the

attic when she was off duty from the hospital, a trustworthy manager of their family finances, a loving mother to their two children, and, also worthy of mention, his private secretary and scribe whenever he was too tired or bored to put on paper some of the tedious scenes and situations he witnessed through the slats.

When he wished to avoid taking pencil in hand, he would dictate his observations to Donna, who knew shorthand (having learned it in high school), and soon she would supply him with a transcript that he would later copy in his own hand and include in The Voyeur's Journal.

Donna also assisted him in compiling the facts and percentage figures that he posted in his annual report, bringing to this task the same high standards in accuracy that she maintained when jotting down medical data at her hospital.

Since Gerald Foos was frequently carried away by fantasies of his significant scientific status, imagining Donna and himself as white-coated colleagues of the renowned couple that ran the Masters & Johnson Institute in St. Louis, his written report often conveyed the professional tone of a sexual therapist or marriage counselor, particularly in the final sentences that formed his "Conclusion." A typical "Conclusion" appeared at the bottom of what he wrote about a romantically disengaged older couple from Joplin, Missouri, who chose to stay in Room 7, one with two double beds.

Since I did not have anything better to do, I decided to observe this unattractive couple. Upon check-in, I noticed that the husband didn't show any emotion. He was an auto factory manager in his mid-40s, 5'8", well-groomed, wore glasses. His wife was also in her mid-40s, slender at 105 lbs, and she had a small mouth. As they entered the room, I noticed that the husband had the same grim expression he had in the office. She went first to the bathroom, then came out and said: "Let's go to dinner."

They came back at 9:30 and discussed a movie they had seen, and she proceeded to undress, taking off her bra by pulling the back around to the front, and then putting her nightgown on first, and then pulling the bra out from beneath. They retired to separate beds while watching TV. Much later he moved over to her bed and attempted to fondle and caress her; but when his wife became amorous it seemed to kill any prospect of his getting an erection.

His wife said: "You haven't been able to do anything in three weeks, so why do you continue to try doing it from this God-damned motel room?"

He made no reply.

She went on to say: "When men kiss and love their wives, they are supposed to get hard, and you don't anymore. I think you're just getting old and don't need sex anymore. And I don't either. So, don't worry about it."

She decided to take a bath, and closed the door behind her. The husband returned to his bed without any expression on his face, but tears began falling down his cheeks. He wiped off the tears, pulled back the covers, and the Voyeur watched as he placed one hand on the head of his penis, and the other on his testicles, and then stroked his penile shaft very quickly. After two or three minutes using this technique, he obtained a large erection, and using a proper degree of pressure and stroking speed, he had an orgasm. The ejaculation was not copious in semen content, so it appeared that he masturbated frequently.

During masturbation, he continued to carefully monitor the bathroom door, I assume to ascertain that his wife wouldn't come out unexpectedly. He wiped the semen on the under portion of the spread, and pulled the covers up.

His wife returned from taking her bath, and silently entered her bed. He retained his silent poker-faced attitude, and then turned off the TV, and then the light, and soon the couple had retired for the evening.

Conclusion: After observing many different forms of impotency, the Voyeur is convinced that this is one of the least discussed and most closeted subject in the sexual realm. This man is not impotent—he may just have a fear of performance, and if his wife were more educated sexually, she probably could cure his "impotency" immediately by giving him oral sex or using her hand on his penis.

She probably comes from a background that frowns on any type of sexual foreplay. The couple will probably remain forever entrenched in this confusion and ignorance.

At a later date, another couple registered to stay in Room 7 with its separate beds—but, unlike the sad husband from Joplin and his dreary wife—these more recent entrants into the Manor House Motel immediately enhanced the premises with their attractive appearance, their general congeniality, and their obvious display of mutual affection—which delighted the Voyeur as he signed them in (*for a total of six weeks!*), and therefore looked forward to seeing an abundance of lusty images of marital bliss, and the opportunity to add some flaming pages to his too-often tepid journal.

The dark-haired slender husband was an Air Force officer attending a six-week long summer training session at the Lowry Air Force Base in Denver, and his wife, a grammar school teacher in Mississippi, was spending her vacation weeks with him here, although (as I soon discovered) she was left alone in Room 7 most of the day.

She was a well-proportioned brunette in her late 20s who was very lively and friendly; and one day, noticing a sign in our office seeking to hire a maid, she volunteered for the job.

"I'm used to working," she explained, "and I'm bored here with nothing to do."

So I hired her as a temporary worker, and she was excellent. She was efficient, cheerful, and never complained. Since she was often around the office, I had many opportunities to talk to her about her upbringing and background. She was born in a rural community in Mississippi and her folks were tobacco farmers. In her cute Southern accent she described a girlhood of much poverty, but she worked her way through college and became a teacher. She met her husband in college, they married early, and he immediately pursued a military career. She professed to being happily married. She did not have children.

As I observed them at night, I could confirm that they seemed to be happy. He was always polite and considerate, and she was as cheerful with him in the room as she was around the motel doing her

*chores. But what completely confused me was the couple's inactive
sexual life. During the first three weeks they were in Room 7, I never
saw them have sex. And yet they were nothing like the other sexually
remote married couples I've watched, arguing and disagreeing so
much of the time. No, the Mississippi couple seemed to be genuinely
fond of one another.*

*Once the husband was overheard mentioning that as a couple
they hadn't had intercourse in some time, but she said, "Whenever
and whatever you want, Sweetheart, it is okay with me." But,
after that, nothing more was said, and nothing seemed to happen.*

*Except late one afternoon, during their fifth week, after she
had completed her maid's work, the Voyeur noticed her lying nude
in the middle of one of the beds. The twin lamps on either side
of the bed were on, highlighting every curve of her young body.
Then, as if in a trance, she got up from the bed and pulled open a
small suitcase in the closet. She groped inside and came out with a
battery-operated vibrator. It was about six-inches long and flesh
colored. She picked it up, brought it back to the bed, turned it on,
and began to slowly apply it to her ribcage, then down over her flat
stomach, and finally it came to rest between her thighs. As the tip
of the vibrator touched the lips of her vagina, shivers of delight
seemed to pass through her entire body.*

*The Voyeur watched from six or seven feet above, hearing her
breathing at an increased rate, and detecting her special smell as she
approached an orgasm, and the Voyeur was also wondering if her
husband was aware that his wife used a vibrator and also traveled
with one. If not, how did she manage to conceal it so well at all
times? And where had she obtained it? The Voyeur wished he could*

have asked her these questions, unveiling mysteries about this sweet and accommodating woman and the man she chose to marry.

Later she got up from the bed, placed the vibrator back in the suitcase, and headed for the bathroom. She filled the tub with water, poured in an ample supply of scented oil, scrubbed and cleaned her body, and also washed her hair. After drying her body and powdering with a perfumed talc, she plugged in her hair-dryer and blow-dried her hair. She took special care in making the curly waves fall flatteringly into place. As she applied her lipstick, she paused a moment to study her naked body reflected in the dressing table mirror.

She then selected a dark blue skirt and white blouse from the closet. After she finished dressing, she tucked some money into her pocket and departed from the room.

The Voyeur left the observation platform and returned to the office. She was there to obtain change for the soft drink machine. She and the Voyeur exchanged pleasantries and a brief conversation. The Voyeur noticed that she was more beautiful at eye level than from the observation vent.

"I'm going downtown to do some shopping," she said. "If you see my husband, would you tell him I'll be back at around 6 o'clock?"

Conclusion: Unfortunately for this couple, they appear to have different levels of sexual intensity. He is probably a two, and she is a seven. Because of this difference, and despite their courteous behavior toward one another, real difficulties loom in the future for this marriage.

NINETEEN

GERALD FOOS took great pride in the fact that he was never caught, that his secret was never discovered. But there was at least one instance when he came dangerously close to exposure.

Up in the attic one day, watching a couple who had been staying in the motel on a weekly rate, Foos saw the husband look up at the ceiling and heard him ask his wife, "What is that vent for? That isn't a heat vent . . . I'm a construction worker and I would recognize it."

"What is it, then?" she asked.

"It could be a peephole."

His wife giggled. "You mean someone could be watching everything we do?"

He said, "There are a lot of weirdos in this world." Then he added, "I'll find out."

Gerald records "feeling somewhat apprehensive at the pro-
ceedings going on below." He cautiously backed away along the
attic floor, left, locked the door, and went back to the office.

In the office he pondered the severity of what he had heard.
From the first, his plan, if discovered, was to call the observation platform a "'service walkway,' i.e. to service electrical wiring, heating pipes, plumbing access, etc. . . . The vents were
used to disperse smoke and bad odors from the rooms. This is
what the subject would be told if he suspected anything out
of the ordinary, and then the burden of proof would be placed
directly on him."

"The next day, I didn't know what to expect," Gerald wrote,
"but I thought perhaps the subject might call the police to
investigate, or that he would confront me personally. He did
neither."

Gerald "stayed completely away from the observation tower
for several days, and tried to determine what the subject was
contemplating."

"After about four days, I ventured up to the observation platform and noticed that the subject had taped the vent shut with
paper. However, there was a small crack on one side, which en-
abled a partial observation. On this particular evening, they
were engaged in an oral sex routine, which later evolved into
intercourse."

Two days later, the wife came to the office and told Gerald
that her husband had gone back to their home state and she
was going to follow him shortly. "At this time," Gerald wrote,
"she revealed some startling facts to me: namely, that [her

husband] had climbed through the vent into the ceiling and walked around. He was a very small man, and was just barely able to get through the vent. I never thought it was possible for anyone to get through the vents, other than a small child. I explained to her that it was strictly a service area platform and she accepted this without question."

TWENTY

DESPITE HIS privileged position as a secret observer of intimate moments, full knowledge of human behavior remained elusive for the Voyeur. A "terrifically attractive couple from Oakland," whom he checked in to a room furnished with two separate beds, added to his sense of wonderment.

He was a handsome 6'3" male of athletic proportions in his late 20s, and she was a 5'8" brunette in her early 20s. They had been living in Boulder, Colorado, the last six months, and now they needed a room with a kitchen for a few weeks until their new apartment in Aurora was ready.

From conversation I learned that she was a former Miss California and a runner-up in the Miss America pageant, and they apparently were married shortly thereafter. Her husband became her agent after the pageant, and he continues managing her modeling career. They are interested in Aurora because of a small

movie company located here and some personal connections associated with it.

But this beautiful couple represent one of the strangest relationships I have observed. After watching them for more than
two weeks, it is amazing—they have absolutely no sexual contact.

They sleep in separate beds. Only career subjects are discussed
in their daily and nightly conversations. They are in disagreement
much of the time. He wants her to more actively pursue her career
in modeling, but she is resistant to the many booking opportunities, or other appearance dates, that he has set up for her. He often
leaves the room angrily and doesn't return for hours.

When he is gone she remains in the room alone, watching
television, and sometimes walks around nude, taking great interest in her body in the mirror, and sometimes sits down and takes
special interest in looking at her legs and feet. She also lies on the
bed sometimes gently caressing her body in different areas, but
I have never seen her masturbate. I can sometimes detect expres-
sions of displeasure on her face, and also at times her body seems
to shudder. It's as if she's shaking off something or someone
that is close enough to touch her. Once I did notice her crying,
which lasted for a few minutes, and then she stopped and seemed
profoundly pacified.

Conclusion: The Voyeur finds it hard to believe that this man
she is married to is only interested in furthering her modeling
career, but from observations this is certainly a consideration.
Again, he has absolutely no sexual desire for this beautiful subject. Perhaps he is a homosexual. But still there are other couples
I have seen who are non-sexual. Not as attractive as this couple,

but youthful non-sexual couples do exist in greater numbers than the general public is aware of.

In fact, my observations indicate that many of these non-sexual couples, not yet in middle-age, generally appear to be contented people. I have developed figures dealing with sexual frequency, and it is as follows:

★ *12 percent of all observable couples at the motel are highly sexed.*
★ *62 percent lead moderately active sexual lives.*
★ *22 percent are of low-drive sexually.*
★ *3 percent have no sex at all.*

Because of no other way to measure this correctly, I have concluded a couple to be "highly sexed" if only one partner is aggressive. But more often than not, in this 12 percent category, both partners are likely to qualify as "highly sexed," and as an example of this I cite a married couple from Wichita, Kansas, who share the single bed in Room 6.

The husband is a white male of 6'2" in his early 30s, and his wife is a 5'8" blonde with fair complexion and a pleasant disposition. I checked them into Room 6 at 5 p.m. In the office they were both very talkative and outgoing. The first thing the husband asked me as he signed in was:

"Where's the best restaurant around here to get lobster and steak?"

Later, from the observation walkway, after they had returned from the restaurant, I watched her go to the bathroom, leaving the door open.

He stood close to her in the bathroom doorway, and, even as she sat on the toilet, she reached toward him and began stroking his penis from outside his trousers.

He smiled, asking: "Are you horny again?"

"I'm always horny," she said, and, as he got closer, she unzipped his trousers, took out his penis, and began giving him oral sex—while still on the toilet. She was an expert fellatrix. She made him have an orgasm, while standing up, in less than five minutes.

"I can taste the garlic you had for dinner in your come," she said.

"Well," he said, "you almost sucked my stomach out."

Later in bed, while watching TV, she was constantly holding or stroking his penis, which remained flaccid. But after she put it in her mouth, he obtained another erection. She then mounted him in a female superior position and controlled the motions until she had what seemed like a super orgasm. He didn't have an orgasm at this time, but then he changed to a male superior position and he did have an orgasm, his second in the last two hours.

Conclusion: This wife definitely possesses a high sex drive. She has no hang-ups and her husband is apparently sufficient for her. Probably a good marriage and happy situation, if he can keep her satisfied. They are a super interesting couple. I wish they had stayed longer.

TWENTY-ONE

THE DISAPPOINTMENT the Voyeur experienced from some guests, like the gorgeous but sexually mismatched couple, was swept away by the joy he took in witnessing moments of unmitigated abandon. A husband and wife from Texas—they said they were on vacation and only passing through—beguiled the Voyeur: she was a ravenous woman who knew what she wanted and left no doubt; he was a partner complicit in the pursuit of pleasure.

The husband was a casually dressed 6-foot figure of about 195 lbs, while the wife was a stunning redhead of about 5'4" with a well-rounded body and a large mouth. The Voyeur eagerly anticipated an intimate view of this couple, but was also disappointed when he noticed at the desk that they both carried packs of cigarettes.

The Voyeur hates smokers because the smoke rises and floods the vent and becomes a tremendous nuisance. There should be strict laws to protect the non-smokers so that his rights are continually violated, but unfortunately there are no measures against this in the state of Colorado, and, in the privacy of their motel rooms, guests do pretty much as they wish.

From the observation platform the Voyeur watched as the couple entered the room. After they had unpacked their luggage, arranged their things and departed for dinner, the Voyeur entered their room briefly to check on the female subject's bra size, and it was 34D.

The Voyeur, in order to authenticate his journal, will from time to time enter a room to determine and ratify his observations in order that accuracy is maintained. The Voyeur is very thorough and secretive in his activity, and no guest has ever discovered that their private sphere was penetrated or intruded upon. As stated many times in the past, the Voyeur is proud of this skillful accomplishment that no observable, or non-observable, guest has ever been damaged or suffered mentally because of the vents. This was a prerequisite on the part of the Voyeur, and without the guarantee of non-discovery the observation laboratory would not have been developed and maintained.

Except for the female subject's large breasts, she looked small and pretty. The Voyeur couldn't believe a woman could appear so delicious and athletically in good shape despite her approaching middle years. She removed her skirt and panties. There was an abundant quantity of hair on her pubic region, which was light red.

She relaxed on the bed beside the male subject, and placed her fingers on the upstanding hard flesh of his penis. She began to stroke and caress it carefully, seemingly not wanting to hurt his manhood. Her mouth slowly opened, and then she began with her fellatio—her tongue making continuous circles, licking the phallic organ up and down, lapping up the front end of the penis and down the underside. She licked on the right side, then on the left side. The top, the bottom, the head, then the base. And when she had completed coated his penis with saliva, she completely inhaled his penis deep-throat style, totally. His body shuddered and shivered as her mouth continued to absorb him.

He then stroked the bulbs of her large breasts tenderly, so that the pores of her skin seemed to open to his fingers, and then he dug in more roughly as he began to move his loins in time with her caressing mouth. He slithered down, his penis slipping from her salivating mouth, and he gently separated her legs, as his tongue trailed downward toward her vagina.

"That's wonderful," she said, "Do it. Lick me, lick me."

She uncontrollably tossed her head from side to side, and her hands found his head and her fingers became entangled in his hair, as she spread her thighs wider and lifted them higher. The cords of her neck stood out as she shouted, "Oh, oh, oh," and then she reached a whimpering orgasm. The male subject immediately entered her in the male superior position, and after a quick series of strokes, she yelled, "Fill me up with come, fill me up!"

He complied and had a tremendous orgasm, and then collapsed on top of her.

Then after about five minutes, he eased his penis out of her and rolled over on his side of the bed. Later he got a towel from the bathroom and they cleaned their sexual organs. The Voyeur's nostrils twitched, smelling the arousing odor of completed sex. But then the male subject fumbled with his clothes until he found a pack of cigarettes. He lit two, passing one on to her. She sucked the smoke into her lungs, and sighed heavily, as if to say: "Sex is over for now, and now we're back to reality and have to deal with the futility of living."

Conclusion: Here are a sexually educated and liberated couple who demonstrate the totality of their love for one another, utilizing sexual style to the maximum. They indicate to all the ability to unchain the sexual inhibitions and ignorance that have imprisoned many individuals. The Voyeur was impressed with their sexual passion but wished that it had not filtered up to him through their cigarette smoke.

TWENTY-TWO

TRENDS AND fads frequently found their way into the rooms of the Manor House Motel. Thanks to Polaroid's portable, folding SX-70 model—considered so revolutionary it appeared with its creator, Dr. Edwin Land, on the covers of both *Time* and *Life* magazines in 1972—instant photography was one such trend. "The advent of the Polaroid camera has had a dramatic effect on the lives of certain individuals," the Voyeur wrote in his journal, noting that he had "observed subjects from all walks of life utilizing the Polaroid camera to record sexual activity," though it was "extensively the sexual desire of the male rather than the female."

But in one memorable instance, the Voyeur watched a very attractive young woman, a college student waiting at the motel for the start of the quarter, who took pleasure in the act of watching herself.

She is white, 21-years-old, 5'6", about 115 lbs, with green eyes, red hair, and creamy complexion. The Voyeur has been observing her for three days and during this time she has called no one on the telephone, and no one has visited her. She apparently knows no one in the area because she is a new student at the Colorado Women's College in Denver, and other than leaving the room to get something to eat, she usually spends all her time in the room reading books, watching TV, and, unfortunately, smoking.

Lonely as she seems to be, she is not shy about her body because she often walks around in the nude. She actually takes great interest in looking at all parts of her body in the mirror. While watching her yesterday, she removed the mirror from over the dresser and placed it next to the wall by her bed so she could watch herself masturbate.

She does so in the following manner. First she stimulated her clitoris with the third finger of her right hand and then appeared to become excited. She then used a long ruler to stimulate both nipples at once (with one hand), passing the ruler back and forth over her erect nipples. She had her legs wide apart—her knees bent out and her back arched. She did not move much when she masturbated other than to observe herself in the mirror, almost like it represented someone else.

When she reached orgasm, her hips raised and her toes clenched downward. Within ten minutes she repeated this, and had another orgasm. When orgasm approached, she would lick her lips, and the appearance of a sucking grimace would be on her face.

Observing her this evening, I notice a more depressed individual than before. Her hair is messed up and she has been releasing gas at random and without shame. I assume she would never do this if anyone else was in the room.

Finally, on the third night, she places a long distance phone call to someone in Wisconsin. It may be parents or other family relatives. She tells them that she is fine, is looking forward to school, and is on her way out to a party. There is no party, of course, but she sounds sincere. As she is talking she is also picking her nose and wiping it on my bedspread. After she hangs up, I see her pacing back and forth, and there are tears in her eyes.

Then she returned to the bed, watched TV, and lit up a cigarette.

Conclusion: She is having a difficult time, obviously, adjusting to the new environment in Denver, and depression and loneliness appear to have overwhelmed her. But masturbation seems to fulfill some of this void, at least temporarily. After observing many subjects, my survey concludes that women have a tendency to masturbate more out of depression than anything else. Men masturbate purely for physical release. This particular female subject, masturbating in front of a mirror, is getting a second perspective—and I, in the attic, a third.

TWENTY-THREE

THROUGHOUT HIS time as resident voyeur at the Manor House Motel, Gerald Foos frequently had occasion to reflect on the Vietnam War. From the tender, careful lovemaking of the wheelchair-bound serviceman's wife, to the lonely older war widow buying the services of a prostitute, his guests led him to offer a consistently critical take on the effect of the war.

It was not just their bodies or their families that were affected, however; the mercilessness of two pilots, their callous reveling in destruction, disturbed him, even while their sexual activity reinforced his thinking on voyeurism.

I assigned Room 6 to a good-looking couple from the town of Rangley, in northwestern Colorado. The man was blond and handsome and stood about 6 feet, and the female was at least 5'8" with long brown hair and large oval eyes. In conversation he told me he was attending a reserve meeting in Denver—he had been a pilot in

Vietnam—and his lady friend was employed somehow at the community college in Rangley.

They also said they were going to be joined later by a friend, also a pilot, and he would need a room. So after I got his name, I booked him in Room 7, right next to the couple, where there are connecting doors.

By the time I'd gotten up to the observation platform, the woman was taking off her ski boots and stockings, and leaning back on the bed.

The blond man was in the bathroom, complaining of a headache, and he said: "I need to get something to eat. It'll make me feel better."

So she put on her boots and they soon left the room, returning to it in an hour or so. Not long after they got back, there was a knock on the door. It was their friend, a tall dark-haired man in his late 20s. After a warm greeting at the door, he came in and then the three of them sat around for an hour or so talking, even though the TV continued playing all the time.

The men talked mainly about flying, with some references to helicopter missions in Vietnam. The man who was booked in Room 7 even recalled once throwing a Viet Cong soldier out of his gunship. The subject makes me sick.

The blond guy in Room 6, who apparently is now working somewhere in Colorado as a flight instructor, described in detail his favorite sport, which is chasing and shooting coyotes from his aircraft. He also said he liked to chase them in the direction of a 500-foot cliff and watch them topple over to their deaths. "Those coyotes become so preoccupied and frantic in trying to elude the plane that I'm able to drive them over the edge, and what a thrill to see them tumble end-over-end and crash into the canyon."

At about 11 o'clock this disgusting conversation ended. The dark-haired guy got up to say good night and went to Room 7. The couple in Room 6 began taking off their clothes. She was absolutely stunning. She was tall and very slender, but the pair of breasts jutting out from beneath her ski sweater made her look anything but slender. Finally, she was nude. But before he joined her in bed, she asked him to turn off the TV and room lights, which he did.

I hurried down from the observation deck toward the parking area and my car. But since every parking space in front of No. 6 was occupied, I could not get my car lights focused on the couple's room, which was now in total darkness. But as I passed No. 7, I saw through the curtains that their friend had opened up his side of the connecting door and he had an ear pressed against it, listening to whatever bed sounds were coming from the couple's room next door, and he also had his pants down and his penis in his hand.

Returning to the platform, I watched him through the vent, continuing to listen as the woman's voice was groaning with pleasure in the dark, louder and louder, as her partner is making love to her. I couldn't see any of it, of course, but she was really loud, and as I shifted to peek down on Room 7, I could see this other guy, standing with his head pressed against the door, masturbating to orgasm.

Conclusion: This observation makes a truism out of my contention that all men are voyeurs to some degree, and will demonstrate this capacity if given the opportunity. But this man, and his fellow pilot next door, disgust me. Their disregard for animals, and the throwing of that Viet Cong individual out of the gun-ship, it makes me hope that somehow these two men will meet the fate of those coyotes.

TWENTY-FOUR

T HE MOTEL was a place where guests retreated to act out their kinky desires. The Voyeur observed one man, a married father of two, having sex with one of the many teddy bears he had brought into his room. "Apparently he only practiced his unusual depravation when he was on the road, away from his family," the Voyeur wrote.

In another far more common encounter, the great diplomacy of a woman turned what could have been an ego-shattering night of embarrassment and disappointment into one of gratification.

A dignified and neatly-dressed white man, probably in his late 30s, standing about 5'8" and weighing at least 175 lbs, explained that he was here on business from Kansas City and needed a room for only one night.

Standing next to him was his attractive 25-year-old companion who seemed to be of Spanish origin but spoke perfect English.

I placed them in Room 11, which has double beds, and gave them about ten minutes to settle themselves before I went up to the platform to see and hear their situation.

He was on the phone when I arrived, speaking loudly while sitting on the side of the bed. The Spanish woman was unpacking a suitcase placed on the other bed.

"My wife and I just arrived," he said. "We've just checked into this motel, and we can meet you at the restaurant we mentioned at 7 o'clock. Is that okay?"

The party on the other line, a woman, said it was okay, and that she and her husband looked forward to it.

After hanging up, the Kansas City man turned to his companion and said, "Now, look, let me do all the talking, and let's just go along with whatever they want, okay?"

"That's fine," she said.

"And don't forget: this couple thinks you're my wife, and so be careful what you say. Also, don't be concerned about any of the extras they may want because I'll make it up, financially, okay?"

"Fine," she repeated.

The man seemed edgy and nervous about the impending meeting with this other couple. He explained to her that he knew nothing about them except they lived in Denver and had advertised in a swingers' magazine. "We'll see what they're like at dinner, and, if we all get along, we'll come back here, okay?"

They left the room shortly before 7 p.m., and a little after 9 o'clock they returned. About five minutes later, I saw a late model Cadillac pulling up at the curb in front of Room 11. Returning to the attic, I noticed that this newly-arrived couple were both in the mid-40s and both were well-dressed and refined looking, especially the wife. She had a face of classical beauty, with an aristocratic nose, high cheekbones suitably attenuated, a fine chin, a long neck, very large eyes and a complexion any model would envy.

But after she had taken off her clothes—and the visiting couple were quick about it—I saw that her breasts were very small, and sagged. After her husband became nude, and the Spanish girl also, the three of them lay on the bed and began fondling one another.

The man from Kansas City was in the bathroom, with the door closed, and when he came out he seemed to be surprised to discover that the others were not only nude but were already in bed stroking one another.

"Wow," he exclaimed, still fully dressed, "so soon!"

As he slowly began to take off his clothes, he watched as his Spanish friend was beginning to perform fellatio on the other man, while the latter's wife kneeled next to them, softly massaging her husband's testicles. The Spanish girl had dark skin, the color of rich chocolate, and her large breasts were ringed delicately with chestnut-brown nipples, and below was her dense forest of curly black pubic hair.

The Voyeur found her incredibly beautiful, and exciting to watch, too, especially as her tongue moved around the purple knob of the man's penis. The latter's wife, while still keeping her hands on his testicles, nodded toward the Kansas City fellow in a gesture for him to join them.

After all his clothes were off, he did move onto the bed with some hesitation, feeling as he did the wife's hand on his scrotum as *well. But nothing she did with her hands, or later with her lips, could arouse his limp penis.*

He was clearly embarrassed, but he did accept the wife's invitation to lower his head between her legs and participate with his tongue, which he did perfunctorily; but his penis remained unresponsive, reducing him to being a mere spectator after the wife shifted her attentions toward her husband and the Spanish girl in a threesome on the other side of the bed—where, in the next ten minutes, each gained an ample degree of satisfaction.

The Voyeur watched all this through the vent, feeling sorry for the subject from Kansas City. That poor fellow surely hoped, after he'd made all these arrangements, that he'd become more than just a spectator.

After the swinging couple from Denver had put on their clothes, had said good-bye, and departed from the room, the man from Kansas City said softly to his companion: "I just couldn't get turned on by this swinging situation. Maybe it's just not for me."

"Oh, don't worry about it," his companion said. "I'll turn you on."

"I'm sorry, but I feel bad," he went on.

"Don't feel bad," she said. "We don't need that kind of sex."

She then lavished maximum attention on his penis, and tongued it to a rigid straining stalk of excitement. She never pulled her hot mouth away from his surging penis until he had ejaculated into her, which he later called: "the best orgasm I ever had."

Conclusion: From what I picked up from all their conversation, the man from Kansas City often takes his Spanish girlfriend with him on business trips. He used this particular trip to experiment for the first time with swinging couples. He obviously could not get, or did not want, his wife to participate in mate-swapping, and the girl served as a substitute. Because people, especially married men, tend to be bored by routine sex with one partner, swinging serves a purpose. But the fact that this man failed to achieve an erection will probably discourage his participating in similar meetings in the future.

The Voyeur, as of this date, has not observed enough group sex in order to hypothesize on the effects of mate-swapping on the marriages of the participants. Whatever the effects, this variance will continue to be practiced by certain adults and should be condoned.

TWENTY-FIVE

VOYEURISM FOR Gerald Foos was a "predictable divination. He had no other choice." He wrote that it made him "feel credible and worthwhile."

"The Voyeur feels strong and brave in the observation laboratory but doesn't feel particularly overpowering anywhere else, and his strength and courage when he is not in the observation laboratory comes from the excess energy remaining from having just been there."

Up beyond the vents, he saw himself as something of an explorer in uncharted waters, "what the majority of people fear and deny in themselves. The taboos. The secrets. The devils and demons. The sexual unknowns. The curiosity. Someone has to be delegated the responsibility to confront these tangible existences and tell other people about them. Herein is the intrinsic essence of the Voyeur."

But in the thousands of sexual encounters he watched, there were some that he found difficult to witness.

I checked in this family from a rural area in upstate New York, putting them in Room 11 on a weekly rate. The space consists of two double beds, and a small nine-by-twelve attached kitchen. The family consisted of a white male and wife, both in their mid-forties—he a 225-pound laborer of sloppy appearance, she a slim woman of average looks and mild-mannered. They were accompanied by their 17-year-old son, a long-hair type, and a 14-year-old dark-haired daughter who is pretty and well-proportioned for her age.

During routine irregular observations, the Voyeur has witnessed this family as enduring while suffering from a crisis of not having enough money to completely satisfy their needs. The father has just commenced working on construction jobs, but the cold and inclement weather, including snow, is playing havoc with his employment on a steady basis.

The wife is working and is receiving just enough money in order to pay the room rent.

The family is arguing and complaining at regular intervals. They need more room with privacy, which represents a constant consuming jeopardy in their lives. They were evicted from their last home for non-payment of rent, and their previous landlord has possession of all their household furniture and belongings.

The adults' sex life is non-existent partly because of their problems and also their lack of privacy. Their son and daughter are not attending school, and have been sitting around the room smoking dope while their parents are away at work. Additionally, the teenaged son has been buying drugs from a pusher in the neighborhood, and this pusher also wants him to sell dope for him at the schools in the vicinity.

The Voyeur reported this plan to the local police department, but they inquired into how the Voyeur determined this situation and knew it was for real. The police said they couldn't do anything because all the evidence was hearsay, and it is not good enough. Of course, the Voyeur could not disclose how he had discovered the plan.

Approximately one week after the family had moved in, the Voyeur noticed one afternoon the teenaged boy and his sister had finished playing a game of scrabble at the kitchen table, and then they moved to the bed to watch television. For the next twenty minutes, after they had smoked some dope, the conversation turned sexual and he began touching her around the shoulders and forced his hand on her breasts. Then he lowered her bra, exposed her breasts, and pushed her back on the bed.

"You're going to do it to me, aren't you?" she asked. She seemed not to be alarmed.

"Don't you want me to?" he asked.

"Not today," she said. "It's too late, and Mom and Dad may come home early."

"No, they won't be coming home yet," he said, "and it won't take me very long."

He pulled her trousers off, then reached in his billfold for a rubber, but she said: "I really don't want to do it now."

Despite her objection, he removed her trousers and panties and soon was entering her body. He grabbed her legs and placed them over his shoulders, and then he shoved himself into her.

"It hurts," she cried. His groans mixed with her cries were very audible to the observing Voyeur. After five minutes of heavy thrusting, he reached an orgasm.

The two of them remained close together for a while, still in a position of intercourse. She then pushed against him, wanting him to get up. He removed his penis as the rubber slipped off, but part of it remained inside her.

"Hold still," he said, pulling the condom out.

"You lose it in there all the time," she said.

After taking hold of the condom, he flushed it down the toilet. She immediately pulled on her panties and trousers. He came back to the bedroom, lay beside her, and they returned to watching television.

Conclusion: The family in Room 11 stayed one more week, and then departed for a destination and dismal future unknown to the Voyeur. The couple's son and daughter, tender in years and yet fully engrossed in the drug culture and sexual permissiveness of the 1970s, suffer immensely by not attending school and being allowed to sit around all day smoking dope. The most common form of incest is probably brother-sister, especially in poor families where children of different sexes must share the same bedroom.

TWENTY-SIX

IN THE Voyeur's annual report of 1977—and specifically on the Thursday evening of November 10, 1977—there was reference to a situation in which the Voyeur saw, for the first time in his life, more than he wished to see.

What he saw was a murder.

It occurred in Room 10.

He described the occupants as an attractive young white couple who had rented Room 10 for several weeks. The male was a slim six-footer of about 180 pounds in his early twenties. The Voyeur deduced from his eavesdropping that the male was a college dropout and small-time drug dealer. The female was a well-proportioned blonde with a 34D-22-36 figure. The Voyeur had checked and verified her bra size after entering the room while the couple was elsewhere.

The couple exhibited a vigorous sex life, indulging in oral sex and intercourse on at least a nightly basis since moving in, and an approving account of this was noted by the Voyeur. Also described, however, were incidents in which drugs were sometimes sold to people visiting Room 10, and, while the Voyeur was upset by what he saw, he never considered notifying the police. In the past he had reported the presence of drug usage and trading (most recently in the case of the teenager in Room 11 who was having sex with his sister), but the police took no action because he would not identify himself as an eyewitness to his complaint.

On the afternoon of November 10, 1977, however, after noticing that drugs were being sold in Room 10 to a few young boys, one of whom appeared to be no older than twelve, Gerald Foos wrote in The Voyeur's Journal:

The Voyeur was angry and decided that he himself must take action to stop this dealer in Room 10 from selling more drugs.

After the male subject left the room that afternoon, the Voyeur entered the room. He knew exactly where the drugs were hidden. The Voyeur, without any guilt, silently flushed all the remaining drugs and marijuana down the toilet. There were approximately ten bags of marijuana and many other assorted pills, and they all went to their watery grave.

This satisfied the Voyeur, and his only remaining wish was that he could appear in the million or so other places where drugs exist, and destroy them also. The Voyeur had accomplished the elimination of other drugs that he had seen other dealers selling, but these villains had never suspected the Voyeur. They just vacated the premises of the motel, thinking the drugs had been misplaced or someone of their immediate acquaintance had stolen them. They did not notify the police or complain. They simply left the motel without knowing what happened to their perilous commodities.

In describing this latest situation unfolding between the male subject and female subject in Room 10, the Voyeur is going to be very brief and only state that the male subject had blamed the female subject for taking his disappeared drugs. After fighting and arguing for about one hour, the scene below the voyeur turned to violence. This was a horrible experience, very offensive and startling—the white male struck a blow to her head, which apparently stunned her, and she yelled: "You hurt me, don't do that," and he replied: "Where are my drugs, you bitch? Tell me, or I'll kill you." She said: "I don't know! I didn't do anything with them."

He didn't believe her, and continued to hit her in the face. Then, suddenly, she kicked him in the groin area, and he really got mad. The male subject grabbed the female subject by the neck and strangled her until she fell unconscious to the floor.

The male subject, then in a panic, picked up all his things and fled the vicinity of the motel.

The Voyeur in observing from the vent, and without doubt, could see the chest of the female subject moving—which indicated to the Voyeur that she was still alive and therefore O.K. So, the Voyeur was convinced in his own mind that the female subject had survived the strangulation assault and would be all right, and he swiftly departed the observation platform for the evening.

After the Voyeur arrived at the motel office he carefully considered what he had observed, and upon reconsideration he definitely concluded that the female was alright, and, if she wasn't alright, then he couldn't do anything anyway, because at this moment in time he was only an observer and not a reporter, and really didn't exist as far as the male and female subjects were concerned.

The next morning, the maid who was cleaning rooms rushed into the motel office and said that a woman was dead in Room 10. The Voyeur immediately called the police, who began an extensive investigation. The Voyeur could only provide the name of the male subject who occupied the room with the female subject, his description, make of car, license number, and that he was in the room with the female subject the evening she was killed. The Voyeur could never provide information that he actually witnessed the male subject's assault of the female subject last evening.

The Voyeur had finally come to grips with his own morality and would have to forever suffer in silence, but he would never condemn his conduct or behavior in this situation.

After the police had checked out their leads, they returned to the motel to report:

The information was bogus. The suspect was using a fake name, a fake address, and a fake license plate on a stolen car.

When I read this account in New York a few years after I'd visited him in Aurora—and nearly six years after the murder—I was shocked and surprised. I thought that the Voyeur's detached and irresponsible response to the fracas in Room 10 was similar to the behavior of New York crime witnesses when a twenty-eight-year-old bar manager named Kitty Genovese was

being attacked by a man with a knife on a street in Queens
shortly after 3:00 a.m. on March 13, 1964.

Although some facts in this case were later disputed—among
them that the initial estimate of thirty-eight murder witnesses
was an exaggerated number—there was no dispute that several
people in Queens saw at least part of the brutality from their
apartment windows, and that none of them rushed down into
the street in time to rescue or assist the young woman who
would soon bleed to death. The *New York Times*, which broke
the story, quoted one unidentified neighbor as saying that he
told another neighbor to telephone the police because "I didn't
want to get involved."

Gerald Foos's explanation in his journal—he was "only an
observer and not a reporter," and he "really didn't exist as far
as the male and female subjects were concerned"—were expla-
nations that didn't surprise me because of his often-expressed
notion that he was a fractured individual, a hybridized combination of the Voyeur and Gerald Foos, and he was also desper-
ately protective of his secret life in the attic. If the police had
grilled him and decided that he knew more than he was telling
them, they might have obtained a search warrant to explore his
property, including his attic, and the consequences could have
been catastrophic.

I telephoned Foos right away to ask about the situation. I
wanted to find out whether he realized that, in addition to witnessing a murder, he might have in some way caused it. He
was reluctant to say more than he had written in his journal,
while reminding me that I had signed a secrecy agreement. He

might have also reminded me that I was now a coconspirator in whatever crimes he had committed. I spent a few sleepless nights asking myself whether I ought to turn Foos in or continue to honor the agreement he had asked me to sign at the baggage claim in Denver in January 1980. But even though he had in some way caused the young woman's death years before by flushing the drugs, had failed to stop the boyfriend as he strangled her, and had callously failed to call for help until the next day because he claimed to see her chest rising and falling, I did not believe Gerald Foos was a murderer. And he had told the police all he knew about the identity of the drug dealer and his girlfriend—who it was now too late to save.

I filed away his notes on the murder along with all the other material he had mailed me earlier in the year. I now knew all that I wanted to know about the Voyeur.

When I learned about the murder I was busy researching a book that would soon take me out of the country. I planned to write about the late nineteenth-century and early twentieth-century immigration of Italians to America, a story that would include the personal experiences of my grandparents and parents as well as my own boyhood recollections of growing up on the Jersey Shore during World War II, while my father's two younger brothers were in the Italian army trying to resist the Allied invasion.

In 1982, having finished interviewing my parents and other relatives who had settled in the United States, I took an apartment in Rome, and later in southern Italy, to learn about the lives of my kinsmen who had remained in their homeland. In the winter of 1985, I rented a house for five months in Taormina, Sicily, to begin writing the book that would be published years later as *Unto the Sons*. Joining me in Taormina was my wife, Nan, an editor at Houghton Mifflin who remained active with her firm in Boston while doing her reading and editing in Sicily; and among our occasional houseguests were our twenty-one-year-old daughter, Pamela, then an intern with the *Paris Tribune*, and our eighteen-year-old daughter Catherine, a sophomore at Bard College.

But throughout these years, from the 1980s through the 1990s, whether I was in New York or overseas, the mail continued to bring me personal greetings and attic-observed information from Gerald Foos in Aurora, Colorado. He reported that the police had so far failed to track down the man who had killed the woman in Room 10, but that the police had been summoned to his Manor House Motel for other matters.

He mentioned that one male guest had committed suicide, shooting himself with a pistol. He noted that a 500-pound guest had suffered a fatal heart attack and that his body, bloated overnight, could not fit through the doorway and therefore the room's main window had to be removed in order for the body to be carried out to the coroner's vehicle. One guest, a married father of two, died confronting a burglar. The fight woke up his family, who heard the gunshot that killed him. Gerald Foos also reported that another guest had died while masturbating, collapsing with his fingers so rigidly clinging to his penis that the ambulance crew was obliged to carry him away in that condition.

In addition to these happenings, Gerald Foos complained of being privy to many other unappealing or appalling examples of human behavior, including robbery, incest, bestiality, and rape—and, even among so-called consenting couples, instances of sexual exploitation. Gerald Foos believed that the legalization of the birth control pill in the early 1960s, which he favored despite being a practicing Roman Catholic, encouraged many men to expect sex on demand. "Yes, the pill allowed women to control their fertility," he conceded, "but she also assumed most of the responsibility, and the blame, if she accidentally became pregnant. The man in her life would ask, 'Have you taken your pill, darling?' and then assume that the issue was settled: for him it was a green light for sex, a quick orgasm, and deep sleep. Women had won the legal right to choose but had lost the right to choose the right moment."

In the years when his parents were a courting couple, as well as when he himself was dating Barbara White in high school, Gerald Foos singled out the fear of pregnancy and the illegality of abortions as big factors in minimizing premarital intercourse. If unmarried couples became pregnant, in most cases it was considered morally obligatory, if not mandatory under a statute, to authenticate the relationship with a marriage.

Gerald Foos said that as a seventeen-year-old farm girl, his mother, Natalie, had been practicing the rhythm method with her boyfriend, Jake, but had "made a mistake"—and thus she was five months pregnant with Gerald on her wedding day in 1934. Gerald went on to say that while the availability of the pill and the redefinition of moral standards in the 1960s helped to phase out "shotgun" marriages in America, he was not sure that the Sexual Revolution had produced anything that refuted his negative recounting of what he saw from his attic and reported in The Voyeur's Journal.

Between the 1970s and 1980s, our country went to war with one another. They had battles with words and images, through law and politics, over what made men and women full citizens of the nation. Across two generations, they argued and fought over everything from women's role in the job market, to their attempt to control reproduction, because of the pill, and from men's role as breadwinner to whether they could love each other and marry, and other things and issues like gender, sex, and family.

During many nights' observations of subjects below the vents, the Voyeur could confirm again and again these on-going quarrels between women and men, which were characterized by unhappy sexual relations and interactions, while at the same time little seemed to be going right as they referred to their responsibilities and jobs in the outside world. When in bed together they lay there for hours watching TV. When men were alone they watched TV and masturbated. Women when alone masturbated too, although not as much. But I think both sexes are now masturbating more than ever. The only couples who seem to enjoy pleasing one another in bed, and to have the patience and desire to give one another orgasms, are lesbians.

TWENTY-SEVEN

ON MATTERS of personal hygiene, integrity, and honesty, the Voyeur gave high marks to few guests. Once he slipped a porno magazine into the table drawer of a room where a visiting minister and his wife were registered. Later, discovering the magazine while his wife was out of the room, the minister quickly masturbated to the centerfold photo and then tucked the magazine into his briefcase. He later complained to his wife about the "filthy" magazine that someone had left behind, vowing to return it to the office with his complaint—but he never did.

On another occasion, two presentable young women in their midtwenties arrived at the front desk asking Donna if they could have a look at a room prior to registering. Normally this was against motel policy, but Donna ignored it and handed them a key. As the Voyeur watched from above, the women hurriedly entered the room and rushed directly into the bathroom, both "desperate to relieve themselves" because of all the beer they'd admitted to having earlier at lunch.

While one woman sat on the toilet, the other squatted over a plastic wastebasket in front of the sink. As the second woman finished and stood up, she accidently knocked over the wastebasket with the heel of her shoe, sending an abundant amount of urine streaming along the bathroom floor and out onto the rug of the bedroom. At first, both women seemed too panic-stricken to move. But then, after mopping up some of the urine with towels, and tossing the towels under the bed, they made a quick exit, returning the key to Donna with the explanation that they would return later. Before they drove off, however, they were met by the Voyeur in the parking area, who politely but firmly invited them back to the room to resume the chore of cleaning up.

Although he was very unhappy whenever he saw male guests urinating into bathroom sinks, which men did routinely when they were a room's single occupant, his anger was also directed at the toilet industry's designers and manufacturers, who were apparently unable or unwilling to address the challenges men had in directing their urine stream accurately while standing in front of a standard household toilet, which is about shin high for most people and has an oval-shaped bowl measuring approximately ten-by-thirteen inches. Urinating into it becomes even more chancy in the morning, the Voyeur explained, because many men, and especially young men, get out of bed with erections.

"You cannot piss straight if you have an erection," he explained, "and that's why so many men prefer the sink, which is about waist-high and offers a wider target area. If I had my way, I'd design a household toilet that was more like the upright urinals you have in the men's rooms of public buildings. There would still be a bowl in front to sit on, but in the back there would be a wide-sized toilet cover that, after you lifted it up and pushed it back in an upright position, men could piss against it and allow their urine to rebound off it and cascade down into the bowl."

But he found it difficult to offer excuses to motel guests whose offensive habits consisted of eating fast food out of containers and then wiping their greasy fingers on the bed linen, and also pet owners who failed to fully wash away the room's rug stains caused by their urinating and defecating dogs.

He faced a dilemma whenever a guest approached the registration desk accompanied by a dog. Should he falsely claim that there were no available rooms and therefore lose business to one of the competing motels, all of which were pet friendly? Should he instead assign them to one of his twelve rooms with vents, and then keep a close eye on their animal's toilet manners?

The problem with his being a dog's watchdog was that dogs often seemed to become aware that he was watching from the attic. Being very keen of hearing and sensitive to smell, dogs would frequently point their noses up toward the vents and begin to bark, causing the Voyeur, while leaning over a vent, to freeze in that position and try not to breathe. If a dog continued to bark, and indeed jumped up and down on the bed while balancing its body on its hind legs, the Voyeur would crawl backward as soundlessly as possible, hoping that his retreat would pacify the animal and encourage it to abide by the masters' admonishments to stop making noise.

But aside from the presence of pets and bathroom violations, the Voyeur's main complaint as a motel owner—a complaint he expressed in letters, journal notes, and occasional phone calls—was the conviction that most of what he saw and heard while he spied on his guests were words and phrases and personality traits that were repulsive, misrepresentative, hypocritical, falsely flattering, or completely dishonest.

"People are basically dishonest and unclean; they cheat and lie and are motivated by self-interest," he commented, continuing, "They are part of a fantasy world of exaggerators, game players, tricksters, intriguers, thieves, and people in private who are never what they portray themselves as being in public." The more time he spent in the attic, he insisted, the more disillusioned and misanthropic he became. As a result of his observations, he claimed to have become extremely antisocial, and when he was not in the attic he tried to avoid seeing his guests in the parking area or anywhere around the motel, and in the office he kept his conversations with them to a minimum.

As the Voyeur's correspondence and voiced comments kept harking on the familiar theme of his alienation and agony, it occurred to me that he might be approaching something close to a mental breakdown; and I sometimes imagined him in terms of the psychotic anchorman in the 1976 film *Network*, who implodes: "I'm mad as hell, and I'm not going to take this anymore!" I was reminded as well of certain literary works from long ago: John Cheever's 1947 story in the *New Yorker* "The

Enormous Radio," in which a couple's marriage slowly suffers as their newly purchased radio mysteriously allows them to overhear and become affected by the conversations and secrets of their neighboring tenants; and Nathanael West's 1933 novel, *Miss Lonelyhearts*, in which an advice-dispensing newspaper columnist becomes an unstable, irascible alcoholic due to his frustrations and sensitivities vis-à-vis his readers' empty lives and dubious solutions.

Except, in the Voyeur's case, I believed his criticisms of other people were expressed without any sense of irony or self-awareness. Here was a snooper in the attic claiming the moral high ground while scrutinizing and judging his guests harshly, and, at the same time, appropriating for himself the right to pry with detachment and immunity.

And where was I in all this? I was the Voyeur's pen pal, his confessor, perhaps, or an adjunct to a secret life he chose *not* to keep completely secret. Maybe he needed me as a confidant in addition to his longtime business partner and wife, Donna. He said that when he first confessed to Donna about his boyhood prowling outside the bedroom of his aunt Katheryn, Donna had been too astonished to reply. She had merely giggled.

Then she went on to ask, "You really mean you did that as a kid? And isn't that what is called a 'Peeping Tom?'" He replied, "No, it's a trip in my exploration," and later he expressed to her his desire to buy a motel and convert it into a "laboratory."

This was early in their marriage, and, after he had found the motel he wanted, he approached her and asked, "Would you go along with me in this? We would have to keep this a secret—just you and me, and nobody else. This is how it will have to be." Donna thought for a moment, and then answered, "Of course, and this is how it will be."

But obviously the solo relationship with Donna was not enough for him, and in time I was invited into his privacy and through the mail I became an outlet—reading his version of what he saw and what he felt, and also sharing some of the personal grief and sadness he experienced as a family man. He wrote to me about the continuing problems of his teenage daughter, Dianne, and on more than one occasion he unburdened himself in letters and phone calls about his college-age son, Mark, who he said spent three months in jail after he and fellow students were arrested for holding up a restaurant, presumably for drug money.

"Mark never did drugs in high school, as far as I know," he told me. "During his first year in college, he did fine. But the second year it seemed he got involved with some real jerks, smart jerks, and they performed an armed robbery. Why? Mark had a brand-new truck, he had all the clothes he wanted, he had all the money he wanted, he had his whole college paid for. And he goes out and commits robbery! Is that a reflection on his family's values? Is that his dad's fault? His mother's fault? Mark had such great potential. He was studying to become a petroleum engineer, where the starting pay is about $200,000 a year. And so he and his friends rob a restaurant! They got forty-seven dollars."

TWENTY-EIGHT

DUE TO my frequent travels between Italy and the United States during these years, I was sometimes months behind in our correspondence, and it occurred to me often that I would be wise to discontinue. What was the point of all this back-and-forth letter writing? Gerald Foos was not my literary property. He was not a subject I could write about despite my continuing curiosity about how it would end. Would he ever get caught? If he did, what would be the trial strategy of his attorneys? Was he so naive to think that jurors could be convinced to accept his attic as a laboratory in quest of truth? And moreover, if the prosecutors had discovered our correspondence while rummaging through his files, might I be subpoenaed to testify?

I would do everything possible to avoid this, of course. But even if he continued to avoid detection, he served no purpose to me as a writer because, as mentioned earlier, I insisted on using real names in my articles and books. I was not a fiction

writer who made up identities and created situations. I was a
nonfiction writer who imagined nothing and gained whatever
I got from talking to people and following them around. I hid
nothing from my readers—real names and real facts that could
be verified, or no story.

Still, whenever the mail arrived bearing his return address
on the envelope, I opened it without delay. And it was with
shock and dismay that, after receiving a letter from Gerald,
dated March 8, 1985, I learned that Donna was dead. She had
died on September 27, 1984. She had been in her late forties
and suffering from lupus.

"It has been almost two years since I've had any contact with
you," Gerald's letter began, and, although I did not perceive an
incriminating tone in his words, I wondered why it had taken
him almost half a year to pass on the sad news. Maybe he had
written me earlier and my houseguest in New York had incor-
rectly forwarded it to me in Italy. In any case, Donna was dead
and Gerald's letter went on to provide me with additional information: "There is a new woman in my life."

I immediately called Gerald from New York to express my
condolences about Donna, and then I followed days later with a
letter asking about this new woman's knowledge of the Voyeur
as discreetly as I could: "Does your present lady friend have
any sense of your interesting past?"

In time I learned that she did; and, like Donna before her,
she not only condoned his snooping but sometimes joined him
in the attic to participate. I did not learn this all at once; in
fact, it would take dozens of letters, several conversations on

the phone, and years of polite inquiry on my part, to piece together a summary of Gerald Foos's life that extended from my
one and only personal visit with him in 1980 to my receiving
his letter in 1985 informing me of Donna's death.

His "new woman" was a buxom five-foot-four, green-eyed divorcée with reddish hair named Anita Clark, and she was eighteen years his junior. Born in Nebraska to working-class parents,
she came with them to Colorado when she was seven. After
graduating from high school in Aurora, she held such short-term
jobs as a nanny, a nurse's aid, and a bus girl at a roadside diner. It
was at the diner that she met her future husband, a truck driver,
whom she married in 1976 when she was twenty-four.

Three years later the couple was divorced, and, with limited
child support and no job, she struggled on her own to raise
their two young boys, the older one having been born crippled.
One of his legs was missing at the knee, the other at the foot.
As he turned five, Anita was living with him and his three-
year-old brother on food stamps in a trailer park.

While taking the boys for a ride in a Radio Flyer wagon one
afternoon along East Colfax Avenue, she noticed a man standing on a ladder changing the lettering on the Manor House
Motel's sign near the entranceway. In response to her cheerful
greeting, Gerald Foos climbed down and engaged her briefly in
conversation. She introduced him to her boys by name—the
older one was Jody, the younger one, Will—both having red
hair like their mother.

The boys smiled as Gerald reached down to shake hands.
He was disturbed and saddened when he noticed Jody without

complete legs. Gerald said nothing but suddenly remembered watching the legless Vietnam veteran struggling to make love at the motel. Anita interrupted Gerald's lingering silence to say that she had an appointment to keep, and so she excused herself and pulled the wagon forward while Jody and Will turned to wave goodbye.

Weeks would pass before Gerald would see her again, this time at a pool party in a trailer park to which he had been invited by a male friend who lived there. Gerald did not recognize Anita at first, focusing his attentions mainly on her slender and large-breasted body dripping wet in a swimsuit. His aunt Katheryn had been built along these lines, and so had his high school sweetheart, Barbara White, and his wife, Donna. But even after he had been introduced to Anita by his friend, he had not recalled their earlier meeting along the sidewalk with her children until she herself mentioned it.

He was also not feeling very sociable on this occasion. He had decided to come to the party at the last minute merely as a distraction from his difficulties with Donna. He and Donna had been quarrelling for weeks. A day earlier she had gone to an attorney to discuss getting a divorce. Gerald had begged her to reconsider, but she had been angry and unforgiving since learning that he had been having an affair that year with a pretty young woman employed with a public relations agency in Denver.

This had been his first and only extramarital experience in more than twenty years of marriage. He had often desired to stray from his understanding with Donna that he could look, but never touch, and he had even admitted in The Voyeur's Journal to wanting other women. But oddly it had not been at his initiative, but rather the aggressiveness of the public relations woman, that had drawn him into his first affair. After decades as a spectator, and never a player, he had finally met a woman who apparently had her eye on him.

To a voyeur this was a novel and intriguing situation. He had not felt so desirable since his star-athlete days in high school. At first he thought he was imagining the PR lady's interest; it was perhaps a symptom of male fantasy. He could not assume that her friendly manner and well-groomed appearance had anything to do with him personally; after all, it was part of her job to flash a smile and exude amiability while entering motel offices every week and dropping off tourist brochures and information about city-sponsored activities.

Still, when she proposed to Gerald that they make a date for lunch, or meet some evening for a drink, he began to think differently. In all his time in the attic he had never observed a woman quite like this one. She was a polished professional and was discreetly feminine in dress and manner, and yet she was openly seductive and apparently willing to take risks with a man she knew was married. She had even met Donna on occasion. But she also seemed to know when Donna and Viola, his mother-in-law, were out of the office, and only he was behind the desk to greet and converse with her—a circumstance that did, indeed, lead gradually to their meeting one evening in a cocktail lounge on the other side of town, and then to spending a few hours in bed together at a neighboring motel.

These meetings went on for months, and for Gerald it was exciting and unique; he was a guest in a motel with an unmarried woman who seemingly wanted nothing more from him than recreational sex and friendship. The sex was mutually satisfying as far as he could tell, although in a physical sense she did not measure up to his ideal. She was a slender woman with small breasts and little muscle tone. She looked better with her clothes on than off. But she was fun and frisky, and he saw no reason why their dalliance could not go on indefinitely—except that it did end, abruptly, after Donna learned of it.

Gerald guessed that Donna had been tipped off by one of the wives who co-owned one of the motels he frequented; but no matter, Donna had so much specific information about Gerald's whereabouts that he made no effort to defend himself. He promised to end the affair immediately and he did. He did not want to lose Donna.

But she could not be pacified. She was a strong-willed individual whose trust in him had been shattered, and she determinedly proceeded with the divorce settlement that she obtained in 1983. She had already vacated their house on the golf course and resided elsewhere in Aurora. During this time her illness with lupus was worsening, and she was unable to maintain her normal working schedule at the hospital where she had risen to become the director of nursing.

Gerald reached out to her regularly, still with hopes of reconciliation; but as she remained adamant, he eventually gave up and contacted Anita Clark, the red-haired divorcée with the two young sons.

Gerald and Anita began to see one another frequently, and in letters to me he described her as a welcomed source of support and reassurance. "She is calm, gentle and very easy-going," he wrote. "She has also promised to keep my voyeuristic life a secret."

In a later note he characterized himself as a changed man, one of less bereavement and more bravado, "If Anita ever would consider marriage, it will not be from gratitude or devotion but because she has learned to love again, almost against her will. She will need some strong, vigorous thinker, some great man whose will and intellect compels her heart's homage and without whose company she cannot persuade herself to live. She has now met that person in Gerald L. Foos."

On April 20, 1984, Gerald Foos and Anita Clark were married in Las Vegas. In later years, Anita helped with the bookkeeping and management of the motel. At the reservation desk she extended equal amounts of courtesy to each arriving guest, but, following Donna's policy, was selective in assigning the more attractive arrivals to rooms providing viewing opportunities for Gerald.

She had seen pornographic films before meeting Gerald, but after marrying him she became accustomed to witnessing live performances while reclining with him in the attic, sometimes simultaneously having oral sex or intercourse. She easily adapted to the pleasurable routines that he had practiced in earlier and better times with Donna, and, because Anita had no outside employment, she worked full time at the motel and soon was largely responsible for its daily maintenance and bookkeeping.

In the absence of Donna and Viola, Anita hired two replacements in the office and also welcomed part-time assistance behind the desk from Gerald's daughter, Dianne, whenever the latter's health permitted. In addition, Gerald recruited the services of his estranged son, Mark, wanting him to gain managerial experience at a time when Gerald was thinking of expanding the business—which, in fact, he did in 1991 with the purchase of a second motel for approximately $200,000.

TWENTY-NINE

GERALD'S NEXT motel was called the Riviera, and it was located at 9100 East Colfax Avenue, about a ten-minute drive from the Manor House. The Riviera was a two-story building with seventy-two rooms. Gerald installed no more than four faux ventilators in the bedroom ceilings because the motel's relatively flat roof provided only tight crawling space within the attic; and so the Manor House remained his observational headquarters.

"Voyeurs are cripples . . . whom God has not blessed," he wrote. "God said to us, 'You get to observe at your own risk.'" In another letter, drawn from his memories at sea, he wrote, "The Voyeur is likened to a ship's chronometer, a continuous unbroken vigilance or sentinel in a state of alert . . . The Voyeur is one that sits up at night, and continually awake at night or day, waiting for the next observation."

During the Christmas holiday season of 1991, Gerald and Anita visited New York City, staying at a hotel not far from my home. But I did not see them. I had just finished one book and was busy with another, this one a memoir called *A Writer's Life* that took me to Alabama to revisit my student days at the University of Alabama in the early 1950s, and also back to my reporting days in the 1960s when I worked at the *New York Times* helping to cover such civil rights confrontations as the "Bloody Sunday" incident that occurred in the old Alabama plantation town of Selma, on March 7, 1965.

In 1993 I was invited to write for the *New Yorker* by Tina Brown as a writer at large, and one of the many subjects I discussed with the magazine's newly appointed editor was the story of the Voyeur and his motel. Tina was amazed and interested in the story, but I couldn't get Gerald to commit to going public, so it was a nonstarter. It had been over a decade since he had first reached out to me; since I don't keep secrets from my readers, and because I doubted Gerald would ever agree to using his name in print, I didn't think the story would ever be published.

It was while I was in Alabama in 1996, doing follow-up research for *A Writer's Life*, that I received word from Gerald Foos saying that his motel-owning days were over. He was now in his early sixties, and his knees and back were so afflicted with arthritis that it was exceedingly painful for him to climb the ladder and crawl around the attic prior to positioning himself over the louvered apertures.

Anita and I retired on November 1, 1996, selling our last motel, the Riviera Motel, and previously selling the Manor House Motel in August, 1995.

P.O. Box 31450
Aurora, Colo. 80041

373449

RETURN RECEIPT
REQUESTED

CERTIFIED
PI5 3908753
MAIL

SPECIAL DELIVERY
SPECIAL DELIVERY

...ar Mr. Talese:

...ince learning of your long awaited study of coast-to-
...st sex in America, which will be included in your
...on to be published book, "Thy Neighbor Wife", I feel
... have important information that I could contribute to
...s contents or to contents of future books.

...et me be more specific. I am the owner of a small
...otel, 21 units, in the Denver Metropolitan area.
... have owned this motel for the past 15 years, and
...ecause of its middle-class nature, it has had the
...pportunity to attract people from all walks of life and
...btain as its guests, a generous cross-section of the
...merican Populace. The reason for purchasing this
...otel, was to satisfy my voyeuristic tendencies and
...ompelling interest in all phases of how people conduct
...their lives, both socially and sexually, and to answer
the age old question, "of how people conduct themselves
sexually in the privacy of their own bedroom."
In order to accomplish this end, I purchased this Motel
and managed it personally, and developed a foolproof
method to be able to observe and hear the interaction
of different peoples lives, without their ever knowing

Gerald Foos's original
anonymous letter to
Gay Talese, dated
January 7, 1980.

Aunt Katheryn, Gerald's sexual obsession.

Gerald's mother, Natalie, outside their home.

Gerald (left), with his cousin "Tootsie" and his brother, Jack.

Gerald on Waikiki Beach in 1955.

Gerald's first wife, Donna.

postcard from the 1960s of the Manor House
Motel, 12700 E. Colfax Avenue, Aurora, Colorado.

Gerald and his parents in front of the Manor House Motel in the late 1960s.

Manor House Motel

ROCKY MOUNTAIN
MOTORISTS INC.

12700 E. COLFAX AVE.

AURORA, COLO. 80010

2 MI EAST OF DENVER ON
HIWAYS 36-40-287
City INTERSTATE 70-225

GERALD L. AND DONNA B. FOOS, OWNERS-MANAGERS

PHONE 303-364-765

The Manor House Motel, with its peaked roof allowing for the creation of Gerald's "observation platform."

#5 Tee
Peble Beach
1978

Gerald golfing at Pebble Beach in 1978.

OFFICE

NO [illegible]   RING BELL

Gerald behind the motel office check-in desk in the 1970s.

...rald in 1982.

A page from the Voyeur's Journal, compiling sexual acts observed and recorded for 1966.

(26)

Total Sex Acts Observed for year 1966

Total # of Sex act Observed	Hetro sexual white	Hetrosexual Black	Homosex male	Lesbian Female	Single male or Female	Interanal Sex	Kinky or Perversion	Oth Se
46	35	5	0	1	3	0	1	

Type of Sex Act Performed

	# Oral Sex w/wo Intercourse	# Intercourse only	# Masturbating only	Resulting in male orgasm	Resulting in Female Orgasm	
Hetro sexual White	5	29	1	35	7	
Hetro sexual Black	1	4	0	5	1	
Homosexual male	0		1		1	
Lesbian Female	1		1	1		
Single male	1		2		2	
Single Female	2		2			
Interacial Sex	0					

A room in the Manor House Motel soon before it was demolished.

One of the Voyeur's observation vents, patched over.

Anita, Gerald's second wife.

Anita and Gerald in New York at the Waldorf Astoria in the 1990s.

Gerald in front of his second motel, The Riviera.

The Manor House Motel as it was being demolished. The "observation platform" was beneath the peaked roof.

Gerald Foos with his wife Anita and Gay Talese at the site of the former Manor House Motel in 2015.

There was something declamatory, nostalgic, and somewhat heartbreaking about the termination and cessation of the function of the observation laboratory located in both motels. Therefore, I feel I can never return to that protected space, that sacred ground, where only truth and honesty was observed and prevailed. But I feel confident that I have accumulated sufficient physical intensity to continue onward with my life without the presence of the motels and their respective observation labs.

He said that prior to the sale he had personally removed the observation vents and covered the holes in the ceilings "to protect the new owners' integrity and business interests, without prejudice."

He and Anita bought a ranch in Cherokee Park in the Rockies, intending to spend almost as much time there as at their home on the Aurora golf course. He could sometimes walk freely along the fairway without a cane, but his ailing back prevented him from playing the game; and so he and Anita devoted much of their leisure time to fishing together on a nearby lake, or taking motor trips around the region and frequently through the agricultural areas of northern Colorado where Gerald had grown up.

I pulled up in front of a farmhouse, knocked on the door, and, after a teenaged boy had opened it, I explained that I was born in this house. After some conversation, he invited me in. I couldn't remember much because the house had been remodeled, and the only visible memory were the steps leading upstairs. I stood near

*the kitchen window where my mother used to peek out on tip-
toe, and name every bird that visited the feeder, and other birds
by their song. I remember thinking at the time: there are bird-
watchers, there are star-gazers, and there are people like me who
watch people.*

He missed his motels very much, although he tried to
convince himself that it was not his arthritis alone that had
prompted their sale. The motel business as he had known it
would soon be a declining enterprise, he believed. When he
began in the 1960s, moral standards were still quite restric-
tive, and, because of it, the tryst trade was inclined to patron-
ize such places as the Manor House— although he insisted that
he ran his business more responsibly than did most of the "no
questions asked" innkeepers who operated along East Colfax
Avenue and elsewhere in Aurora. He not only asked questions
in trying to verify the identity of incoming guests but also, at
opportune moments, he lifted his binoculars and gazed through
the office window toward the rows of parked cars, noting on his
pad the license plate numbers of each vehicle.

But, in any case, the Manor House and other small motels
that had traditionally drawn numbers of cautious lovers—
"hot sheet" guests, swingers, homosexuals, interracial couples,
adulterers, adulteresses, and others preferring to rendezvous
in places where they could walk directly from their cars into
their rooms without having to pass through lobbies and use
elevators—were people who at this time were just as likely
to register in prominent hotels and well-appointed franchise

motels, most of which had rooms with television sets offering pornographic programs.

Of course, none knew better than Gerald the difference between TV porn and seeing it live from an attic, and this is what he most missed after selling his motels. Often when he drove his car past the Manor House and the Riviera, he would pause along the curb at East Colfax Avenue and, as the engine idled, he would sit staring from afar at what he had long known so intimately and over which he had once presided, in the words of his journal, as "the World's Greatest Voyeur."

He could recall not only the specific positions and angles of multitudes of prone bodies but also their names and their room numbers and what was so special and memorable about them— the lovely pair of lesbian schoolteachers from Vallejo, California; the Colorado married couple in bed with the young stud they employed in their vacuum cleaner distributorship; the beautiful vibrator lady from Mississippi who worked briefly as a Manor House chambermaid; the mystifying Miss America candidate from Oakland who slept in Room 5 with her husband for two weeks without having sex; the suburban mother who enjoyed lusty matinee meetings with a doctor before returning home to dinner with her two young children and her handsome husband; and the happy and horny husband and wife from Wichita, Kansas, about whom the Voyeur wrote in his journal, "I wish they had stayed longer."

Reels of these and similar images rotated through his mind with clarity almost every day and night, undiminished by the passage of time. He remembered the voice of a woman who had called the Manor House more than thirty years ago, in the early summer of 1967, requesting a room for four days.

She said she would soon fly into Denver from Los Angeles, adding that when she had previously stayed at the Manor House the management picked up its guests at the airport. Although this had been a courtesy provided by a previous owner, Gerald told her that he would meet her. His viewing platform in the attic was then in its second year of operation.

At baggage claim he greeted a well-groomed brunette in her early twenties who wore a flowered cotton dress with white gloves and was traveling with a single large leather suitcase. In the car she explained that she had earned a master's degree in education but was thinking of attending the University of Colorado Law School. She wanted to specialize in inheritance litigation, and she went on to elaborate in a clipped and lecture-like manner: "A great fortune is sure to be divided. Death will make it necessary, and surviving heirs will demand it. And distant relatives will urge their claims for a share and very often the law aids their requests. And that is where I want to make an entrance in their lives."

Since this was Gerald's first outside meeting with a guest prior to check-in, he was curious but reticent, wanting to behave properly while chauffeuring her toward what was certainly not proper. Forthcoming as she was about her career aspirations, he did not want to risk offending her with such personal questions as whether or not she was married, or even if she had friends in the Denver area. It was enough that he was interested in what she was saying about the law and other subjects, such as capital punishment—which she declared she opposed, and which he was pleased to tell her that he did also.

After he had pulled into the parking area, and Donna, who was then still his wife, had booked her a room, Gerald headed directly up to the attic and wrote down what he saw.

> *She finally slipped off her lace petticoat, then un-hooked her bra, and her breasts were unusually large, the kind that remain hidden in a tight bra and want to escape. After an hour of thinking quietly to herself while unpacking, and organizing her things, she finally lay nude on the bed and began a routine of teasing masturbation. During orgasm she stretched her legs out and up, and raised her torso.*
>
> *The Voyeur masturbated to orgasm along with her.*
>
> *The next day she and the Voyeur had a brief chat in the office before she took a taxi to the campus, and later that night before going to bed she again masturbated. She did this at least once every day during her four-day visit, and each time the Voyeur joined her.*

When she checked out, Donna hired a driver to take her to the airport while the Voyeur remained in the attic. He did not want to say goodbye. He wanted to retain how he preferred to see her, in the nude, giving pleasure to herself and to him as well. She never telephoned again for a reservation, and he never knew what happened to her; but as far as he was concerned, she was forever his guest, his unaware object of desire, a link in a loop of lovely women whom he had once observed when younger and now reflected on during his emeritus years as a dislodged voyeur.

It might suggest a prolonged fantasized harem on his part but what was fantastic to him was that it had all been real—not drawn from his imagination, but rather what he himself had witnessed. His observations were a veritable slice of life that reaffirmed how incomplete was the picture of people seen functioning and posturing daily in such places as shopping malls, rail terminals, sports stadiums, office buildings, restaurants, churches, concert halls, and college campuses.

For so many years he had been privy to other people's privacy, but now, although myriad secret scenes remained engraved in his mind, he had lost forever the sense of wonder and excitation that used to precede each guest's entrance into a bedroom—the sound of a key turning a lock, the sight of a woman's foot crossing the threshold, the conversation of a couple while they unpacked their luggage, the unhinging of a brassiere, the bathroom visit, the removal of clothing, the lowering of the bedsheets, and, if those were indeed wooing words that he heard, his burning desire to see what would happen next.

He could only guess, of course, and that had been part of the thrill, the not knowing until after it had happened, as well as the surprises and disappointments that were part of the bargain. But whatever he saw nurtured his desire to see more. He was an addictive spectator. His occupation was anticipation. And it was from this that he had retired when he sold his motels.

THIRTY

Between 1998 and 2003, I was spending lots of time in China and elsewhere in Asia, following the fortunes of the Chinese women's national soccer team and one of its players, Liu Ying, a principal character in the book I was working on, *A Writer's Life.*

During this time, and through the following decade, I had more or less forgotten about my voyeur pen pal in Aurora, a city I had never heard of before receiving his first letter in 1980; and after he had sold his motels, my interest in Aurora had entirely vanished—until I surprisingly saw it mentioned on the front page of the *New York Times*, on July 21, 2012.

Under the main headline was a report that a twenty-four-year-old graduate student in neuroscience from the University of Colorado in Denver had fatally shot twelve people, and wounded seventy others, in an Aurora movie theater prior to the midnight screening of a Batman sequel called *The Dark*

Knight Rises. The shooter was identified as James E. Holmes, a product of a middle-class community in San Diego, whose parents were described in the *Times* as "really, really nice people" and whose mother was a registered nurse.

The Aurora police said that Holmes, dressed in black and with his hair dyed orange and red, fired randomly at audience members while using an AR-15 assault rifle, a Remington shotgun, and a .40-caliber Glock handgun. Many 911 calls from the theater alerted the police, who soon caught Holmes near his parked car and took him into custody. He later admitted that he had installed incendiary and chemical devices and trip wires in his unit within an Aurora apartment building.

After quickly reviewing the *Times*'s article and seeing that Gerald Foos's name was not listed among those who had been killed or injured, I finally contacted him by phone after a patient operator had tracked him down at a new address. Foos agreed that he and Anita were fortunate in not attending the screening of *The Dark Knight Rises*, but they had attended movies at the theater many times, and he said that he knew what the shooter's apartment looked like.

"It's the same third-floor apartment on Seventeenth and Paris Street that I'd rented a few years ago for my son, Mark," Foos said. Records show however—yet another example of Foos's unreliability—that Mark Foos actually lived at 1760 Paris Street, a block away from James Holmes's apartment at 1690 Paris Street. "We'd had many heart-to-heart talks there. After I moved my son into another neighborhood, this guy apparently replaced him, although we don't ever recall running into this guy whose picture is now all over the news."

A few weeks later, Gerald Foos was again corresponding with me, and in one of his first letters he described exploring Aurora in the aftermath of the tragedy.

As I drove past the Aurora Mall and the 16 Cinema multiplex, where the shooting took place, and is still under police investigation, I noticed the cluster of flowers and teddy bears that people had placed along the ground in memory of the victims. This is a new area of the city—lots of shining windows and beautiful buildings: the county courthouse is here, the police station is here, the library is here. Why the killings here?

Haven't the people of Aurora treated their fellow men with kindness and consideration, so that the sword of Damocles was lowered on us? Or were the killings just a natural occurrence in our society, which we tolerate?

In another letter, he wrote:

I feel terribly uncomfortable in today's world and society. As the Voyeur I felt particularly overpowering on the observation platform, but now, as Gerald, I do not feel that way anymore. Gerald feels restless in his expansive home, and the feelings of his disappearing youth are present in his mind. As he looks in the mirror above his bathroom vanity, he notices the age in his eyes, and the grey hair on his head and beard. He plans to dye his hair, and after he does he sees it as a sham, an untruth that he is attempting to permeate on anyone that he may meet today. In applying the dye he is doing what the Voyeur always stood against—any attempt to subvert reality, substance, the truth, and instead Gerald is resorting to an artificial illusion that his fellow men may accept as the truth.

In his car Gerald drives through Aurora, and as he approaches East Colfax Avenue he notices the Mexican development that exists just east and west of the Manor House Motel. East of the Riviera Motel, there is now mostly Asian businesses, which took the place of the businesses he used to know. This disturbs him, the knowledge that the people he used to know have either moved away or died. He knows no one on the street or business here. He feels lost and without a city anymore. The barbershop is gone. The gas station is gone. And now the Voyeur and Gerald are separate entities, completely disconnected since their tenure in the observation platform has ended.

At a street corner, Gerald stops his car as the traffic light turns red. While pausing, he looks up through the windshield and sees a camera overlooking the intersection. He knows that his picture has just been taken, and so has the license plate of his car.

Proceeding on to the local bank, where he stops to make a deposit, he passes under another camera that scans the parking lot, and another camera hangs over the entranceway. Inside the bank, as he stands in front of the teller and makes his deposit, he is photographed once more by a camera posted in the ceiling.

Later, while visiting a grocery store, one of the few stores that Gerald has known from previous years and where the manager is a friend, he asks his friend, while pointing up to a camera:

"What do you do with those tapes that are changed every day?"
The manager says, "They're for our security, as you know, but
the police, the FBI and the IRS also make use of them, and we
never know why. All we know is that almost everything we do is
on record."

Gerald gets back in his car, and while returning home he thinks
about all the changes that he and the Voyeur have lived through
since opening the Manor House Motel more than thirty years ago.
Now the private lives of public figures are exposed in the media
almost every day, and even the head of the CIA, General David Pe-
traeus, can't keep his secret sex life out of the headlines. The media
is now in the Peeping Tom business, but the biggest Peeping Tom
of all is the U.S. Government, which keeps an eye on our daily lives
through its use of security cameras, the internet, our credit cards,
our bank records, our cell phones, I-phones, GPS info, our airline
passenger tickets, the wire taps, and whatever else.

Perhaps you may be thinking, why is this of interest to Gerald
Foos?

Because it is possible that someday the FBI will show up and
say, "Gerald Foos, we have evidence that you've been watching
people from your observation platform. What are you, some kind
of pervert?"

And then Gerald Foos will respond: "And what about you, Big
Brother? For years you've been watching me everywhere I go."

THIRTY-ONE

During the early spring of 2013, I received a phone call in New York from Gerald Foos saying that he was finally ready to go public with his story. Many years had passed since he had disposed of his motels, and, while he could not be sure of the legal outcome, he believed that the statute of limitations would now protect him from invasion-of-privacy lawsuits that might be filed by former guests of the Manor House and Riviera motels.

He also was approaching the age of eighty, he reminded me, and if he did not share his journal material with readers now, he might not be around long enough to do so in the future. So he suggested that I fly out to see him soon.

Within a month, after I had cleared my calendar for a four-day visit, I met Gerald Foos for breakfast in the bar lobby of the Embassy Suites hotel near the Denver International Airport.

As he spotted me at one of the tables and called out to me by name, I recognized him mainly by his voice—a loud and familiar voice that I had become accustomed to hearing during our decades of communicating by phone. Otherwise, there was little similarity between this elderly man I saw coming toward me and the Gerald Foos I had last seen in 1980.

In those days he had been a vigorous and compactly built individual in his midforties who stood about six feet, weighed 200 pounds, was clean-shaven, and had a full head of dark hair. Now, as he slowly approached with his right hand extended, he carried a cane and was a balding, gray-haired senior citizen with a mustache and goatee. Tightly buttoned over his massive chest was a wide-shouldered gray tweed jacket and, under it, an orange-colored sports shirt, black trousers, and loafers.

His hazel eyes were covered with tinted glasses that, as he later explained, were prescribed for his nearsightedness. He acknowledged as well that his height had shrunk to five nine and his weight had risen to 240 pounds.

"But I feel fine," he said after we had shaken hands and sat down and began scanning the menu. Then he looked up and, lifting his cane in my direction, said, "I see that you're as dapper as ever," and, with a smile, added, "Is that silk necktie you're wearing the same one that slipped down through the slats that night when you joined me up in the attic?" I assured him that it was a different necktie, but our conversation was interrupted by the arrival of his wife, Anita, who apologized for being late because of her difficulty in finding a parking space.

Eighteen years younger than Gerald, Anita was as he had described her in his letters. She was a petite, quiet, and observant woman who stood five feet four and had frizzy red hair, green eyes, and a voluptuous figure that was notable even though she favored modest attire. She was now wearing a flowered dress buttoned at the neck, and, after her initial greeting, she sat in silence throughout breakfast while her talkative husband outlined our itinerary.

"After we leave here," he said, "I'd like to take you to our home so you can see my collection of sports memorabilia in the basement—tes of thousands of sports cards that Anita has organized in alphabetical order, and we have two hundred baseballs signed by the likes of Ruth, Gehrig, DiMaggio, Williams, Mantle, and so forth, including a rare one signed by 'J.Honus Wagner.' His name 'Johannes' was never referred to after he became famous as 'Honus,' but I have this 'J.Honus Wagner' from the early 1900s that went into packs of Piedmont cigarettes until Wagner, who didn't smoke cigarettes, objected to it. So these cards are rare, as I say, as are the old leather football helmets that Sammy Baugh used to wear, and I also wore in high school. And I have Walter Hagen's clubs, which he used in 1928 in winning the British Open . . ."

He went on to explain that one of the reasons he is now willing to reveal himself as a voyeur is that he might also have an opportunity to call media attention to his sports collection, which he said is worth many millions of dollars, and he was eager to sell it, along with his large house with its many steps that his arthritic knees cannot climb without causing him great pain.

"I'll give away my big house for nothing to whoever buys my collection," he said. His current dream is to live in a single-story home without steps.

I replied that I was eager to see his sports collection, but reminded him that I had flown here for on-the-record interviews about his career in the attic, and we had both already agreed that we should try to learn more about the 1977 murder of the drug dealer's girlfriend in Room 10 of the Manor House Motel.

In mid-March, in fact—at least three weeks before my flight to Denver—I had telephoned Gerald Foos to inform him that, without naming him as a witness, I intended to contact the Aurora Police Department and learn if it had uncovered any new information about the death of a young woman in the Manor House Motel on the evening of November 10, 1977.

Foos did not object to my doing this because he had long regretted his negligence on that evening and believed that in going public with the story, and admitting his failings, he might obtain what Catholics seek when they confess their sins. He said he hoped to achieve some sort of "redemption," especially if his candor revived public interest in the crime and eventually brought the killer to justice—if, indeed, the killer was still alive.

But the Aurora Police Department promptly reported back to me that it had no information about this almost forty-year-old crime, and during our breakfast I showed Gerald Foos copies of the letters I had recently received. One was from the division chief, Ken Murphy, who wrote, "Unfortunately we were unable to find any death/homicide matching your criteria. We found only one homicide in November 1977, but it occurred a couple of miles away from the Manor House Motel." That murder, which remains unsolved, was of a twenty-eight-year old Hispanic woman named Irene Cruz. She was found strangled to death on the morning of November 3 by housekeeping staff in a room at the Bean Hotel in Denver.

The other letter, from Lieutenant Paul O'Keefe of the homicide unit, said, "I have personally checked the Colorado Bureau of Investigations Cold Case webpage, as well as our own internal list of active cold cases, and have found nothing that matches the information you have provided. A review of APD records was also completed for a week to either side of the date that you noted in your letter, and we have found no reported homicides (solved or unsolved) during that timeframe."

Lieutenant O'Keefe recommended that I consult the two county coroner's offices that might have then collected a dead woman's body in the city of Aurora—the coroners in Adams County as well as Arapahoe County—but neither had any information, nor did the third source I checked for statistics and vital records: the State of Colorado Department of Public Health and Environment. The latter would not even consider my request for information, explaining that only family members of the deceased had access to death records. In phone calls, two police officers said it would not be unusual for there to be no paper trail in a murder such as the one I described; the identity of the victim was unknown, and the crime took place before police departments used electronic records.

It is also possible that Foos made an error in his record-keeping, or transcribed the date of the murder inaccurately, as he copied the original journal entry into a different format; Foos often told the same story more than once across his journals and letters. Over the years, as I burrowed deeper into Foos's story, I found various inconsistencies—mostly about dates—that called his reliability into question.

I had received cooperation from the *Denver Post*'s news department, I mentioned to Gerald Foos, but nothing in the paper's 1977 obituary files provided us with a lead.

"It seems as if that young woman just fell through the cracks," he said, but added that this might not exonerate him from legal consequences. In publicly admitting that he had watched the drug dealer murder the woman, and did nothing to prevent it, "I could be an accessory to a crime. It would be a serious deal because I never called the police at the time . . . I might be convicted of second-degree murder charges. Who knows? One attorney told me there's a law called 'circumnavigate' which allows the courts to do a lot of things. It was put into effect because of sex offenders, like priests who offended children long ago, and by 'circumnavigating' you can make it appear that it happened last night."

Still, Foos went on, after years of reluctance, he was now willing to admit the truth. "Life comes with risks," he said, "but we can't be concerned with that. We just tell the truth."

With his cane he pointed up toward a few video cameras that were positioned high above our heads within the hotel's atrium, a vast open space that soared six stories high and re-flected the movement of a pair of glossy glass-sided elevators.

"I noticed cameras posted on the roof outside as I walked in, and others are above the front desk and everywhere else you look around here," Gerald Foos said, repeating his com-plaint about widespread voyeurism that he had already cited in letters. It was of course ironic that he, of all people, would take offense at being watched; but rather than debate the point here, where a waiter was removing our breakfast dishes, I de-cided to delay our discussion until we had our promised on-the-record interview at his home.

THIRTY-TWO

As we stood on the sidewalk in front of the hotel, waiting for Anita to bring the car, he again pointed up to an overhanging camera but withheld comment, noticing that a doorman stood nearby watching him.

Sitting behind the wheel of her four-door blue Ford Escape hatchback, Anita waited while her husband squeezed his large body into the passenger seat, and I climbed in the back, and soon we were headed north along sparsely trafficked country roads bordered by cornfields, wheat fields, and stretches of uncultivated land that Gerald said was owned by speculators and was sometimes invaded by mountain lions, bears, skunks, and badgers, while above were Canadian geese flying in from the north.

Half turned around in his seat, Gerald directed my attention to other things that interested him, such as the lake where he and Anita often went fishing, and the Valero store where they bought gas and Anita knew the manager ("He's from Nepal."), and then we headed toward where the couple lived—a quiet community of neatly paved streets, manicured lawns, cul-de-sacs, rows of blue spruce trees, and high-end residences whose similarity in design made it difficult for Gerald and Anita to relocate their own home after they had first bought it and had driven to a real-estate office two miles away to sign the deed.

"On our way back we spent hours wandering all over this place looking for our house," Gerald recalled. "We kept getting lost in and around all those cul-de-sacs. Finally we saw a guy in the street and I called to him, 'Hey, we bought a house around here but can't find it,' and he said, 'Oh, that also happened to me. Lots of these new houses look alike.' I didn't have a GPS then, but I had the address, and soon this guy sent us in the right direction."

Anita paused before turning into the driveway of a large, modern green house with white trimming and stone facing and spruce trees in front. Gerald clicked a remote that opened the door of a three-car garage in which was parked a white Ford Fusion sedan, and hung along the walls of the garage was an orderly arrangement of household tools and fishing rods and also a mounted deer's head and the bow and arrow with which Gerald said he shot the animal during a hunting trip years ago.

After entering the house from a side door in the garage, Gerald asked Anita to turn off the alarms and the laser beams in the basement, and he told me that his sports collection down there was valued at $15 million. He then led me through the dining area into a large living room with mahogany furniture and an eighty-inch television screen and several tall cabinets along the walls containing some of the eighty dolls that he and Anita had collected during their almost thirty years of marriage. I remember reading his notes describing his boyhood attraction to the dolls he saw in his aunt Katheryn's bedroom, and how his mother diverted his interest from dolls to collecting baseball cards; but it occurred to me that after his marriage to Anita, the latter served as his proxy in drawing him back to dolls and acquiring some of these models I was now seeing in the living-room cabinets and elsewhere in the house.

As I stood next to him, he removed from a glass shelf a red-haired, green-eyed doll wearing a white lace dress and white shoes, and he said, "Anita and I were in Florida, and I had a picture of Anita when she was very young, and they made this doll right off that picture." He went on to explain, "Every one of these dolls you see is totally porcelain, from the feet, through the body, everything," and then he took in hand a pretty blue-eyed, blonde-haired doll measuring nearly three feet and said it was a one-of-a-kind product designed by the German doll maker Hildegard Günzel, who was known to collectors around the world. "We paid over $10,000 for this one," he said.

At my request he pointed out some pictures of his aunt Katheryn that were among the framed photos of family members hanging along the walls. In one photo she is shown standing in a farmyard with her hands on her hips smiling at the camera.

Although she wore floppy trousers and a loose-fitting black lace blouse, the outlines of her curvaceous body were quite evident. There was also a photo near it showing Gerald as a farm boy, holding his dog within view of his aunt's bedroom window. In addition, there were photos of his parents, Natalie and Jake, standing in front of the office of the Manor House Motel; and of Gerald and Anita in the lobby of the Waldorf Astoria during a holiday visit to New York in 1991.

Upstairs, hanging on the walls of his office, were the license plates of some of the automobiles he used to drive—his Cadillacs, Lincolns, Thunderbirds. Encased in one corner of the room, next to his desk, was his gun collection—several rifles, shotguns, and boyhood BB guns; and on a shelf nearby were two German Lugers that he claimed to have gotten from an American colonel who had taken them from the home of the Nazi commander Hermann Göring. There was also a Japanese sword and scabbard that Gerald said he acquired at a home sale.

In a guest room next to his office were more of Anita's porcelain dolls, a doll carriage, several of her Avanti-made stuffed animals, and dozens of glass figurines representing cats and other creatures—a menagerie occasionally joined by Anita's two pet cats. All the women that Gerald Foos had been personally associated with were collectors, he said, adding that his first wife, Donna, had a very large stamp collection and "paid as high as a thousand dollars for one stamp." Anita's interests were not restricted to dolls, he went on, but included a coin collection as well as an accumulation of bottles of Velvet Collection wine from the Napa Valley bearing images of Marilyn Monroe on every bottle.

Ever since the couple had sold their motels, Anita devoted much of her free time to alphabetizing his millions of sports cards (ranging from one depicting Troy Aikman, former quarterback of the Dallas Cowboys, to that of Chris Zorich, a onetime lineman with the Chicago Bears)—an "act of labor and love" on her part that Gerald proudly pointed out to me after we had stepped down into the basement.

Some of the sports cards were placed within the hundreds of photo albums that stood side by side along the multiple rows of bookshelves that lined all four walls of the subdivided basement, which had an eleven-feet-high ceiling and measured seventy-five by forty-five feet in total floor space.

In addition to those in the photo albums, there were hundreds of other cards exhibited individually within small standup acrylic frames that rested on or within the room's many display cases.

As Gerald Foos slowly led me past the cases, he would sometimes pause, take hold of a certain card, and make comments about it.

"Here's a rookie card of Michael Jordan," Gerald said, adding that he purchased it at a flea market years ago from an ill-informed trader for only twenty dollars. Gerald then held up a card showing the baseball player Alex Rodriguez and admitted that it had dropped in value in recent years. "Here's a guy—excuse my English—but he just pisses me off, because if he would have stayed away from steroids he would have probably been the greatest player in the world."

After raising and praising the card of Hank Aaron, and then of Jackie Robinson, and then of the Detroit Lions' Hall of Fame running back Barry Sanders, who played during the 1990s, Gerald held a card that had come with a box of Cracker Jack candy, showing the Pittsburgh Pirates' shortstop from the early 1900s, Honus Wagner. In one corner of the room were dozens of football helmets autographed by NFL stars—Joe Montana, Jim Brown, Len Dawson—and on the other side of the room, lined along four wooden shelves, were two hundred autographed baseballs that Gerald said were worth more than their weight in gold. Among the signatures were those of Joe DiMaggio, Ted Williams, Barry Bonds, Mickey Mantle, Hank Aaron, and Pete Rose. ("He should be in the Hall of Fame.") Each ball was mounted on a small wooden stand with a brass plaque bearing the name of the player who signed the ball, and each ball was covered with a plastic globe that was slightly larger than the ball and protected it from fingerprints and other marks.

Neatly stacked on shelves above the rows of baseballs were dozens of Wheaties boxes, the covers of each featuring a famous athlete, among them John Elway of the Denver Broncos, Roberto Clemente of the Pittsburgh Pirates, and Jerry Rice of the San Francisco 49ers. Some of these unopened cereal boxes, such as the one with Lou Gehrig on the cover, were decades old.

"There must be generations of worms living in some of those boxes," I said.

"Yes, and that makes them more valuable," Gerald replied, with a smile.

THIRTY-THREE

Upstairs, seated across from me in the living room, Gerald answered some questions.

"How would you like to be described in the press after you go public with your story?" I asked.

"I hope I'm not described as just some pervert or 'Peeping Tom,'" he said. "I think of myself as a 'pioneering sex researcher.'" He said he felt qualified to be called a pioneer because he had observed and written about thousands of people who were never aware of being watched, and therefore his research was more "authentic and true to life" than, for example, the material coming from the Masters & Johnson Institute, where the findings were drawn from volunteering participants.

"Why does your writing in The Voyeur's Journal so often switch back and forth between the first and third person?"

"Because I felt that I was different individuals," he said. "When I was downstairs in the office, I was Gerald the

Businessman. When I was up on the observation platform, I was Gerald the Voyeur."

"Did you ever think of filming or tape-recording your guests?"

"No," he said, explaining that to be caught with such equipment would have been easily incriminating, and using it was also impractical. There were often long stretches of time when not enough was happening in the bedrooms to justify the use of a camera or a recording device in the attic. In any case, he never considered the use of such equipment.

Later I asked Foos if he had heard of Erin Andrews, the television sportscaster who was secretly filmed coming out of the shower in her hotel room by a stalker who had altered the peephole in her door. The man, who then posted nude footage of Andrews on the Internet, was convicted of a felony and sentenced to thirty months in prison. Andrews sued him and the hotel for $75 million in damages to compensate for the "horror, shame, and humiliation" she suffered. In February 2016, a jury awarded her $55 million.

Foos had been following the case on the news; his take did not surprise me. "While I've said that most men are voyeurs, there are some voyeurs—like this creep in the Fox Sports case—who are beneath contempt," he told me. "Again, he is a product of the new technology, exposing his prey on the Internet, and doing something that has nothing in common with what I did. I exposed no one. What this guy did was ruthless and vengeful. If I were a member of the jury, I'd unhesitatingly vote to convict."

Back in his living room Foos added, "All I needed up there was lots of patience and the ability to describe in my Voyeur's Journal the situations and trends that I saw below."

He recalled that one of the early trends of the 1970s' Sexual Revolution that was evident at the Manor House Motel was when couples began to undress one another, rather than to change in a bathroom, or with the lights out, as had been the custom in earlier years. Another sign of the '70s' liberation was an increase in his guests' participation in group sex, interracial sex, and same-sex activity, adding that "people began to be freer with one another, sexual relations seemed to be more relaxed, and women began telling men what they wanted, being more open and less shy about it."

He, too, became physically responsive, he said, explaining, "I became more pepped up sexually up there—any man would, any woman would—and so consequently I would come down and Anita and I would have great sex. We always had great sex," he said, nodding toward Anita, who sat nearby. After a pause, she nodded back.

He conceded that he learned a lot about sex from his wives, first from Donna, and then even more from Anita. While he was an obsessive watcher, he had known few women intimately beyond his wives, he pointed out. As a bachelor in the Navy for four years, he had been picked up a few times by bar girls, and during his twenty-year marriage to Donna he had been faithful until the final year, when he had the brief fling with the Denver public relations woman. And he had been faithful throughout nearly thirty years of marriage to Anita, he continued, adding

that what made Anita a compatible partner, in addition to her
loving nature, was her being "visual." By this he meant that,
unlike most women, Anita liked watching other people having sex and also enjoyed viewing porno films. Most women
more preferred being watched than watching others, he said,
which may partly explain why men spent fortunes on porn and
women on cosmetics.

"Only 10 percent of women are voyeurs," he said, "while
almost 100 percent of men are voyeurs." He described Anita as
being among the 10 percent.

"This is true?" I asked her.

"Yes," she answered in a soft voice.

"Yes," he declared, and went on to explain, "I'm not saying
that other women aren't turned on by erotic material. I'm only
saying that men are much more visual, and that women are
more likely to be sexually aroused by reading erotic material in
a book." He recalled having watched many female guests at the
Manor House holding a book with one hand and masturbating
with the other.

"Since you have spent half your life invading privacy, why are
you so critical of our government invading our privacy in the interest of tracking down terrorists and other criminals?" I asked.

"I don't like criticizing the government—it's the only one
we have, and everyone is allowed mistakes," he said, "but I
think we've made too many mistakes. Government voyeurism is now coming out of the woodwork. Big Brother now has
incorporated our lives, our opinions, our thought processes—
we're all being recorded electronically on devices few of us

understand. We just know it's there. I counted twenty video cameras around your Embassy Suites hotel this morning.

"Any justification for this level of voyeurism at the Embassy Suites is nonexistent," he said, and he repeated what he had told me many times in the past: *his* voyeurism at the Manor House was "harmless," because guests were unaware of it and its purpose was never to trap or entrap or criminalize anyone. But he suggested that the government-conducted voyeurism that we know today is essentially an evidence-gathering game; and anyone who actively opposes this invasive technology at this time, in this period of post-9/11 protectiveness, might be regarded as unpatriotic or even treasonous.

"People in power want the status quo," he said, and such people do not want to be exposed as deceitful and duplicitous— which is what the former National Security Agency contractor Edward J. Snowden, managed to do in releasing documents alleging that, for example, U.S. intelligence agencies were even tapping the cell phone of its ally in Germany, Chancellor Angela Merkel.

"Edward Snowden in my opinion is a 'whistle-blower,'" Gerald Foos said. Instead of being driven into exile in Russia, and considered by many to be guilty of treason, he should be praised "for exposing things that are wrong in our society."

"Do you not also claim to be exposing wrongs in our society as you share with us what you described in The Voyeur's Journal?"

"Yes," he said. "And I also consider myself a whistle-blower."

"And what do you conclude from all that you've witnessed?"

"That basically you can't trust people," he said. "Most of them lie, and cheat, and are deceptive. There are many, many examples of this in The Voyeur's Journal, like all those people failing the 'honesty test,' and preaching one thing and doing another. What they reveal about themselves in private they try to hide in public. What they try to show you in public is *not* what they really are—and knowing this has made me very skeptical of people in general. In fact, because of what I learned from the observation platform, I'm now antisocial. I just don't trust people much, and, if I can avoid them, I do.

"Even now," he went on, "years after I sold the motels, I just try to stay away from people. I have no one that I consider a neighbor. Anita and I both try to stay away from our neighbors. We might say hello to them, but we keep our distance. When we go out to dinner, it's just the two of us. Otherwise, I'm a loner."

"But you once described *yourself* as two people," I reminded him. "In the motel office, you said you were Gerald the Businessman. In the attic, you were Gerald the Voyeur. Well, who is responsible for not making a telephone call for an ambulance while that woman lay strangled on the floor of Room 10, on the night of November 10, 1977?"

"If I'd known that this particular lady was dying, I'd have called an ambulance immediately," he said. "I would have said, 'I was walking by the window and heard a scream'—or something like that. Of course, I would not have said that I'd seen it from the observation platform. I'd have said I'd seen it through a crack in the curtain."

This was certainly not the first time that he had remained inactive while witnessing horrible scenes at his motel, he acknowledged. He had previously seen examples of rape, robbery, child abuse, incest, and once he watched quietly while a pimp pressed a knife to the throat of a prostitute until she agreed to surrender money she was accused of withholding. Gerald's journal had mentioned a time when he had telephoned the police to report drug dealing at his motel, but no action was taken due to his unwillingness to fully cooperate as a witness.

He loathed drug dealers in part because he feared their activities would draw narcs to his hotel, but he was especially sensitive to the harmful effects of drug usage following the arrest of his son, Mark. Although it was in a losing cause, Gerald said that in 2012 he voted against the legalization of marijuana in Colorado.

"This drug dealer back in 1977 was selling drugs out of Room 10 to some young students, and one of them didn't look more than twelve," Gerald recalled. "Anyway, when this dealer left the room with his girlfriend, I did what I'd done with dealers before—I flushed the drugs down the toilet. Now when he comes back that night, and can't find the drugs—he'd hidden them in a bag within the registry system against the wall, after removing the screws—he begins arguing with his girlfriend.

"'Who the hell was in here?' he begins to yell, and then he is blaming her, and hitting her, and she's crying, 'I'm your girlfriend—let me go.'

"He kept hitting her, harder, and once she kicked him in the groin and he really got mad and began strangling her. Soon she collapsed and fell to the floor, right in front of the vent. I was looking right down at her, there on the floor, and I kept saying under my breath, 'Don't move, don't move, he might strangle you again.'

"Before he left the motel, he picked through some of her things on the floor, and took some cash and credit cards. 'Don't move,' I kept telling her. He then turned, opened the door, and he was gone. I kept watching from up there, and thought she was breathing, but she was not moving at all. Her eyes were closed, but I swear I saw her chest moving, and I thought, 'Well, she's okay.'

"I quit the observation platform for the night, and went down to the office. Later I told Donna about it, when she returned from the night shift at her hospital. She asked, 'Well, you saw the chest going up and down?' 'Yes.' 'Well, she's probably just unconscious, or something like that. You know, she's going to come around and everything will be okay,' and I said, 'Well, I hope so.' It was very late, and I remember Donna repeating, 'In the morning, she'll probably be okay. We won't say anything, and neither will she. You know, her life's her life, and that's the way things are.' Donna went on to say, 'People come into the hospital all the time, and they've been strangled by their husbands, or they're shot in the head by someone, and it's terrible and . . .'"

He paused, and continued, "The next morning, the maid came to work, and I watched her as she went to the rooms, and soon she came to that room, Room 10, and she opened the door and went in. And all of a sudden she came running out, and I thought, 'Oh, no.' And I knew what she was going to tell me. She told me, 'Gerald, I think the lady in No.10 is dead.' I said, 'How do you know?' 'She's not breathing.' I said, 'Where's she lying?' 'She's on the floor.' Oh, no. She was lying just as I'd last seen her."

He went on: "I called Donna. 'Go over there and check her.' So Donna did, and soon she came back, walking back really quick, and I thought, Oh, Jesus, don't tell me—no heartbeat. And Donna came in and said, 'She's dead, Gerald, she's dead.' I said, 'Okay, we got to call the police. Only thing we can do is go call the police.'

"The police came, and then we had to wait until the coroner gets there, which takes an hour or two. The police just walk around waiting for the coroner, they have to guard the body. Then the coroner shows up in his little panel truck with a helper, and they cover the body and load it up in the wagon and off they go to an autopsy room, and I'm sick and saying, 'You know, I could be responsible for this.' I said to Donna, 'I saw her breathing.' She said, 'I know, you told me.'"

Gerald took a breath and repeated what he had said earlier: "Yes, if I'd known she was dead, I could have called an ambulance and explained that I'd been walking by the window and heard a scream . . . but that's not the way it occurred."

THIRTY-FOUR

AFTER I had returned to New York, I continued to correspond and talk regularly on the phone with Gerald Foos, but not much more seemed to be happening—there was nothing more to add to his story. He had written the final page of his journal. But even though he hoped that his confessions might bring him "redemption," and also expedite the sale of his home and sports collection, I sensed that he was guided by more than just that, and even *that* might be wishful thinking on his part.

How could he assume that his honesty would achieve anything positive? It might just as easily provide evidence leading to his immediate arrest, subsequent lawsuits, and widespread public outrage.

Still, it was possible that Gerald Foos *needed* the notoriety—his ego, especially now that he was so aware of his advanced age and diminishing health, drove him to want to become known for what he had seen and written during his many years as a private observer, and this was more compelling than his fear of being found out. In a way he was like the nineteenth-century rogue and voyeur portrayed in Professor Steven Marcus's book *The Other Victorians*—an individual so taken by the idea of self-exposure or narcissism that he produced a multivolume confession called *My Secret Life*, although he withheld his name from the manuscript. By contrast, Gerald Foos was acknowledging his true identity, taking all the risks, and, while he was giving me what I wanted, I was still not sure what motivated Gerald Foos, who, after all, was a master of deception.

In all his years of snooping he had never been caught. "Because of the extreme cautiousness and concern that embodies the Voyeur," Gerald wrote, "not one subject has ever discovered the complete secret of the observation vents. No one was ever hurt or exposed." And what he communicated in letters and phone calls was not necessarily what he believed, if he even knew what he believed. He was a man of many moods and attitudes, and at times he presented himself as a social historian, a pioneering sex researcher, a whistle-blower, a loner, a double personality, and a critic intent on exposing the hypocrisies and hidden appetites of his contemporaries.

Although the comparison is perhaps inappropriate, since he was not responsible for exposing the corruption of a president, Gerald Foos's eagerness to take credit late in life called to mind the decision by a retired FBI agent named Mark Felt to come forward and admit to being the famed Watergate whistle-blower known as "Deep Throat." In a memoir published in 1979, Felt wrote that he "never leaked information to Woodward and

Bernstein or to anyone else!" But by 2005, when he was nearly ninety-two years old, Felt at last unmasked himself. Felt and his family had argued over whether or not to go public with his identity. A decisive element, according to his daughter, was a wish to profit from the revelation. According to the article in *Vanity Fair* that revealed Felt's secret, she told her father, "We could make at least enough money to pay some bills, like the debt I've run up for the kids."

Yet Felt was conflicted over how the revelation would affect his reputation, and up until the night before, he wavered. It was unlikely that Felt would face any legal repercussions for being Deep Throat, though he had earlier been charged in an unrelated case with conspiring to violate the constitutional rights of Americans. In 1972 and 1973, as an FBI agent, Felt had authorized illegal break-ins at the homes of nine people associated with the Weather Underground, the leftist group. At Felt's trial in 1980, Richard Nixon appeared on his behalf; his testimony was interrupted by spectators shouting out "liar" and "war criminal." Felt was convicted, and ordered to pay an $8,500 fine, but a few months later, he was pardoned by Ronald Reagan. Nixon sent Felt a bottle of champagne with a note: "Justice ultimately prevails."

What charges, if any, might be levied against Gerald Foos? He openly admitted to being a voyeur, although he added that nearly all men are voyeurs. Foos insisted that he never harmed any of his guests, since none were aware of his watching them, and so the worst that might be said was that he was guilty of trying to see too much.

He began as a boy kneeling under windowsills, and then, a half century later, he retired from his louvered life in the attic to exist in a society overseen by street cameras, drones, and the eyes of the National Security Agency.

As a voyeur, Gerald Foos was now passé.

And the Manor House Motel was now passé as well.

THIRTY-FIVE

When Gerald and his wife Anita sold the Manor House Motel in 1995, the new owner ran the place without knowing the history behind the rectangular-shaped six-by-fourteen-inch plaster-board patches that were centered in the ceilings of a dozen rooms. The motel changed hands in 1997, and was sold again during the winter of 2014 to a real estate partnership headed by a seventy-five-year-old Denver-based developer named Brooke Banbury.

Mr. Banbury envisioned replacing the motel with a multi-level apartment house, or a hotel, or perhaps a medical building with a bank on the ground floor. After he had acquired the motel, its contents, and the surrounding land for $770,000 in cash, the Korean occupants promptly vacated their office and living quarters and left behind clothes and shoes in the closets and food in the refrigerator and under the front counter.

There was also a small suitcase secured with a padlock, and when Brooke Banbury opened it he discovered a submachine gun with three loaded magazines and extra bullets. The police were summoned and they did not return the rifle.

Most of the twenty-one rooms in the main building had fresh linen on the beds except for about a half dozen that had been used by guests just prior to the sale and after the departure of the chambermaids.

But a week or so after the sale, while Banbury was standing in the parking area talking to a couple of city officials, a Lexus SUV drove by and pulled into one of the parking spaces. A well-dressed Asian gentleman then stepped out of the vehicle and walked toward a door of one of the rooms, presumably having a key.

Interrupted by the loud voice of Banbury, who declared that the motel was now out of business, the man quietly returned to his car and left. A few minutes later, a second car arrived and parked in the same spot. This time two young Asian women stepped out and were about to knock on the door, but quickly retreated upon hearing Banbury calling to them and waving them away. After staring quizzically at Banbury for a moment, both women turned toward one another and laughed as they drove off.

It was the intention of Banbury's wife, Mary Jo, to donate the motel's contents—the beds, bureaus, lamps, linen, and everything else—to one of the local charities or welfare agencies; but all refused, explaining that they lacked the storage space for such a large volume of material or had insufficient numbers of personnel and vehicles to collect it. So her husband hired a demolition crew for about $30,000 to demolish every-thing and haul it away.

This was accomplished in about two weeks, after which the workmen left a plot of flat land, measuring 100 by 282 feet, that was covered with dirt and small chunks of rock and splinters of wood intermingled with weeds, vines, and strips of electric wiring, all enclosed in chain-link fencing—which was how the property still looked four months later when Gerald and Anita Foos visited it, near the end of the summer of 2015.

Since their home in the Denver suburbs is several miles from Aurora, and they had not recently driven past their old prop-erty on East Colfax Avenue, they were late in learning about the sale and demolition of the Manor House Motel.

There were tears in Anita's eyes as she parked the couple's car on a side street bordering the fence. For a few moments she and Gerald, who sat in the passenger seat, silently stared through the windows of their car out toward the extension of wire netting surrounding the more than half acre of empty space.

"Seems that everything is gone," Gerald said finally, open-ing the car door, and, with the aid of his cane, stepped up to the curb. It was a hot Sunday afternoon and there were no pedestrians and very few motorists moving up and down East Colfax Avenue. After waiting for Anita to join him, the couple then headed arm in arm along the sidewalk toward the open front gate. There was no guard on duty, no warn-ing signs posted, no security cameras in evidence, but before advancing beyond the gate Gerald looked to his left and right to be sure that there was no one in sight who might see him as trespassing.

"I hope we can find something to take home," he said, as he and Anita entered the area and began walking around with their heads down, searching for a memento or two that might be added to Gerald's collection in their basement—perhaps a doorknob, or a room number, or some other small identifiable item.

But the demolition crew had pulverized everything beyond recognition, except for a few chunks of green-painted stone that had lined the walkway along the parking area (Gerald had painted them himself, and he selected two pieces for the trunk of their car) and also a strip of electrical wiring that had been connected to the tall red sign that had spelled out the name of the motel.

"That's where we met," Gerald said, referring to an afternoon in 1983 when, while he was up on a ladder changing the lettering, he had called down words of greeting to Anita, who was then strolling along the sidewalk pulling a wagon bearing her young sons.

"You then also asked for my phone number," she recalled.

"Yes," he said, and added, "It's too bad we didn't get here earlier, when they began wrecking this place. We might have gotten a piece of that sign."

They walked around slowly through the lot for another fifteen minutes, keeping their heads down but finding nothing more of interest.

They were both wearing dark clothes—Anita a black print dress with low-heeled shoes, he a black suit with a white shirt and gray silk tie. Neither was wearing a hat, and Gerald was perspiring and also complaining of fatigue.

"Let's go home," Anita said.

"Yes," he agreed, turning, taking her by the arm and heading back toward the gate. "I've seen enough."

Author's Note

After *The Voyeur's Motel* had gone to press, reporting in the *Washington Post* called into question the dates during which Gerald Foos owned the Manor House Motel in Aurora, Colorado, and other elements of his story, such as how he met his second wife, Anita. I visited Gerald Foos in early 1980, and later that year, Foos sold the motel to a man named Earl Ballard. After publication of the story in the *Washington Post*, which was the first time I had heard of Earl Ballard, I spoke to him and Foos, and both confirmed that during Ballard's ownership, Foos had uninterrupted access to the motel. In August 1983, Ballard sold the motel, and Foos was locked out of the attic until he repurchased the motel in July 1988. Foos then sold the Manor House motel a final time in August 1995.

As I made clear in the first edition of this book, Foos was an inaccurate and unreliable narrator, but he was undoubtedly an epic voyeur. The events Foos claims to have witnessed as a voyeur, the scenes recounted in his Journal and in this book, all took place prior to my visit in 1980 and Foos's first sale of the motel, so he clearly had access all that time. While different versions exist of how Foos met his second wife, the version he related to me is fully plausible. Owing to the reporting in the *Washington Post*, a handful of minor changes have been made to this edition. Otherwise this book remains unchanged.

About the Author

Gay Talese was born in Ocean City, New Jersey, in 1932, to Italian immigrant parents. He attended the University of Alabama, and after graduating was hired as a copyboy at the *New York Times*.

After a brief stint in the army, Talese returned to the *New York Times* in 1956. Since then he has written for numerous publications, including *Esquire*, the *New Yorker*, *Newsweek*, and *Harper's Magazine*. It was these articles that led Tom Wolfe to credit Gay Talese with the creation of an inventive form of nonfiction writing called 'The New Journalism.'

Talese's bestselling books have dealt with the history and influence of the *New York Times* (*The Kingdom and the Power*); the inside story of a Mafia family (*Honor Thy Father*); his father's immigration to America from Italy in the years preceding World War II (*Unto the Sons*); and the changing moral values of America in the period between World War II and the AIDS epidemic (*Thy Neighbor's Wife*).

Gay Talese lives with his wife, Nan, in New York City.